HOW TO VINYL WRAP

Cars • Trucks • Motorcycles

Tyler Copenhaver-Heath, Elliot Hutchens, and Travis Hunt

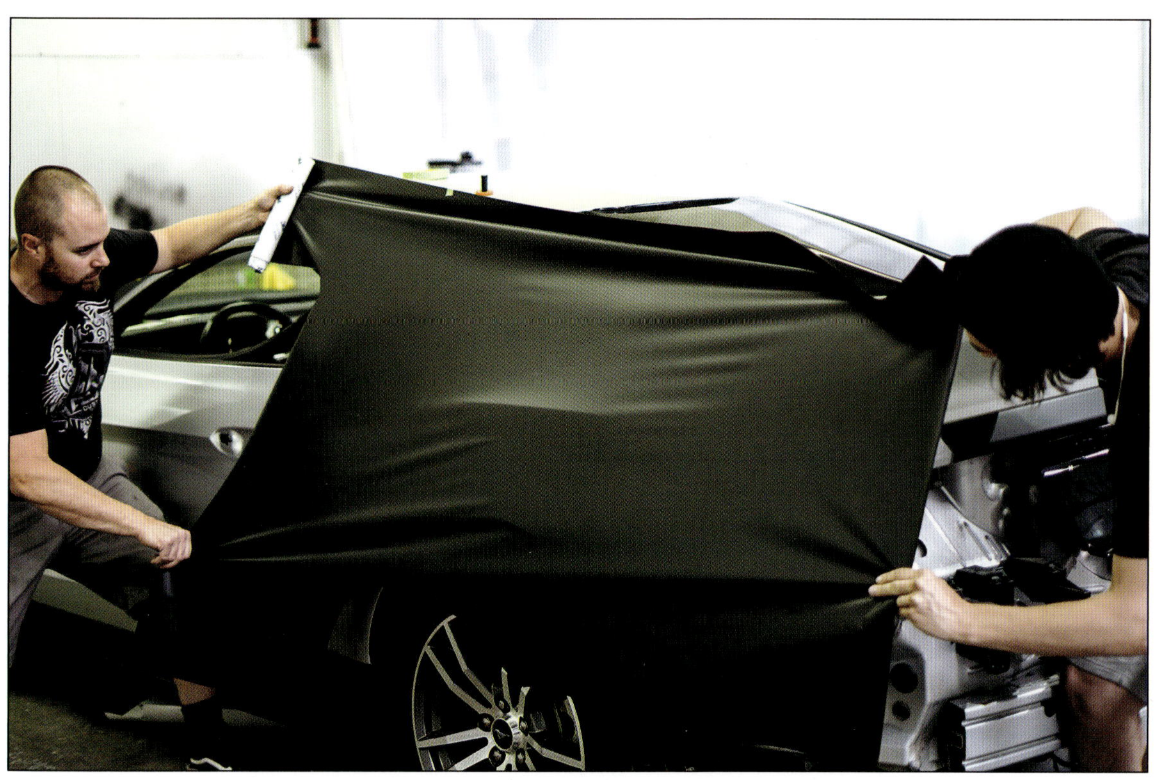

CarTech®

CarTech®

CarTech®, Inc.
6118 Main Street
North Branch, MN 55056
Phone: 651-277-1200 or 800-551-4754
Fax: 651-277-1203
www.cartechbooks.com

Edit by Wes Eisenschenk
Layout by Monica Seiberlich

ISBN 978-1-61325-521-6
Item No. SA473

Library of Congress Cataloging-in-Publication Data

Names: Hutchens, Elliot, 1981- author. | Copenhaver-Heath, Tyler, 1981- author. | Hunt, Travis, 1974- author.
Title: How to vinyl wrap cars, trucks & motorcycles / Elliot Hutchens, Tyler Copenhaver-Heath, and Travis Hunt.
Other titles: How to vinyl wrap cars, trucks, and motorcycles
Description: Forest Lake, MN : CarTech Books, [2021] | "SA473."
Identifiers: LCCN 2021026001 | ISBN 9781613255216 (paperback)
Subjects: LCSH: Motor vehicles–Decoration–Materials. | Vinyl film, Self-adhesive.
Classification: LCC TL255.2 .H88 2021 | DDC 629.222–dc23
LC record available at https://lccn.loc.gov/2021026001

Written, edited, and designed in the U.S.A.
Printed in China
10 9 8 7 6 5 4 3 2 1

Cover: Photo Courtesy Andrew Marshall Photography (andrewmarshallphotography.com)

DISTRIBUTION BY:

Europe
PGUK
63 Hatton Garden
London EC1N 8LE, England
Phone: 020 7061 1980 • Fax: 020 7242 3725
www.pguk.co.uk

Australia
Renniks Publications Ltd.
3/37-39 Green Street
Banksmeadow, NSW 2109, Australia
Phone: 2 9695 7055 • Fax: 2 9695 7355
www.renniks.com

Canada
Login Canada
300 Saulteaux Crescent
Winnipeg, MB, R3J 3T2 Canada
Phone: 800 665 1148 • Fax: 800 665 0103
www.lb.ca

CONTENTS

ABOUT THE AUTHORS

Tyler Copenhaver-Heath

Elliot Hutchens

Travis Hunt

Tyler Copenhaver-Heath was the president of Apex Customs and is a three-time entrepreneur with 18 years in the automotive business. He has an extensive background in sales, promotions, and marketing.

Tyler's bachelor's degree in biochemistry enabled him to study every product that is offered by Apex Customs down to the molecular level. Tyler's deep technical and practical understanding of Apex's products enables him to guide his technicians and customers to make informed decisions about every facet of a customization project. He also has his master of business administration (MBA) degree from Arizona State University's W. P. Carey School of Business.

Elliot Hutchens, the cofounder and former vice president of Apex Customs, is a consultant, technical engineer, marketing executive, accountant, and three-time entrepreneur with 20 years of experience in the automotive aftermarket industry.

He has held various positions in business management, operations, technical systems design, accounting, information technology, and automotive customization. Elliot currently resides in San Diego, California.

Travis Hunt has more than 8 years of experience as a vinyl installer with more than 1,000 completed projects. Specializing in full color changes, he has also created and installed numerous graphic designs, stripe kits, and custom vinyl wraps for both custom and commercial use.

Travis works as a general manager at a premier custom automotive facility, where he trains other vinyl installers how to increase the quality of their installs while maintaining a high level of efficiency.

ACKNOWLEDGMENTS

Tyler Copenhaver-Heath

Thank you to my family: Corey, Nikki, Tracey, Audrey, Bert, and Susie. Also, thank you to our office manager at Apex Customs, Daena Orquiz, for taking some of the weight off me the last few years.

Elliot Hutchens

Thank you to the entire team of employees, consultants, and independent contractors who have helped build Apex Customs and train me in my tradecraft over the years.

Special thanks to my son, Gabriel Archer Hutchens, for giving me the strength and motivation to continuously strive for improvement and take on new challenges.

VINYL WRAP BENEFITS AND USES

This 1964 Chevrolet Impala is wrapped in 3M 1080 Gloss Blue Metallic. The vehicle was a complete build project. Like any other classic vehicle, a lot of bodywork went into prepping the surface for the wrap. It just looks like a flawless paint job with no fisheyes or runs.

and feel of a vehicle in a matter of days with a removable protective coating at a fraction of the cost of traditional paint is a relatively new trend. Changing the look of your vehicle, which used to take weeks and was limited to highly skilled technicians with multiple years of experience, is now available to the average car enthusiast with a limited budget in his or her own garage.

There are a variety of new vinyl-wrap films on the market, and manufacturers are consistently trying to outdo one another to come up with the next crazy thing. Many of us were first exposed to the potential of vinyl wrap through the "chrome craze," as vehicles had bare polished metal (blindingly shiny blue or anodized red). To this day, most of the general

Gone are the days of painted graphics on windows, billboards, and vehicles. Moving into the future, the painters and artists of yesteryear are outshined by high-tech graphic artists and their ability to transform a common work vehicle into a masterful work of marketing art. Chances are good that if you have seen a vehicle and wondered about its crazy color, pattern, or design, it was most likely a vinyl-wrapped vehicle.

21st-Century Graphics

Vinyl wrapping, which is also commonly referred to as vehicle wrapping, has become one of the most popular aftermarket automotive customizations in the 21st century. While the concept of displaying your mark on a car has been around since the early days of the automobile, the ability to transform the look

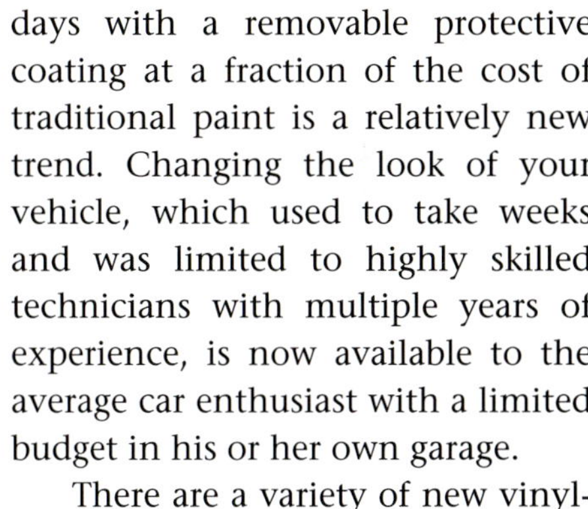

This Jeep wears 3M IJ180 print film with gloss laminate. It was a custom printed and designed wrap just for this vehicle.

public is perplexed about this stuff. How did that car get chrome plated?

However, chrome was just the start. Today, there are a variety of cutting-edge colors and patterns. Cars even display color-shifting films.

For modern enthusiasts, a variety of alternatives to traditional automotive paint is available. New products, such as liquid vinyl, have entered the automotive restyling market in recent years. Even products that have been on the market for years, including rubberized paint and bed liner products, are used for a wide variety of automotive customization applications.

However, no other paint alternative on the market provides the usability, durability, flexibility, return on investment, and ease of removal that vinyl wrap provides.

What Is Vinyl Wrap?

At its core, vinyl wrapping is the process of applying pressure-sensitive sheets of vinyl material to a vehicle's painted surfaces by hand. The process allows you to change the look of your vehicle in a matter of hours in a clean and dry space. The results of a properly installed vehicle wrap look identical to traditional automotive paint. Only a trained eye can tell the difference between a professionally wrapped car and a painted car. While producing showroom-quality results requires experience and expertise, anyone can perform the process of installing vinyl wrap.

Vinyl wrap can be installed on everything from cars, trucks, and sport-utility vehicles (SUVs) to boats, trailers, automotive parts, interior trim, and even electronics. It is reversible and designed to be

Samples of material are shown from left to right: dull (matte), slightly glossy (satin), and gloss similar to an OEM paint job. Each material has its place in the custom film industry. Black can be a great accent piece to a full wrap, and, depending on the car flow, one of these finish options may look better than the others. Remember to look for the flow in vehicles. Manufacturers spend millions designing vehicles. Sometimes it's best to go with the flow (design) and just tweak the details.

removed from the surface of a vehicle at any time and without damaging the paint surface. The material used for a wrap is essentially a large sticker or decal. With an average thickness of 3 to 4 mil, vinyl wrap provides a protective layer that will keep your factory paint job safe from road debris, harsh weather elements, and even vandalism.

The sheets of vinyl applied to the vehicle are available in a wide range of colors, patterns, and textures from a variety of manufacturers. Vinyl wrap is available in every color combination that you can imagine from primary colors to neon pink. In addition to an extensive color selection, each automotive vinyl manufacturer also offers a variety of patterns, finishes, and textures. Finishes range from matte, gloss, chrome, and satin to carbon fiber, textured, and color-shifting.

While each vinyl manufacturer provides varying levels of quality, durability, ease of installation, and cost, vinyl wrap generally provides a life span of five to seven years. Beyond the brand of material for the vinyl wrap, the life span of the final product is impacted by weather, climate, how the product is cared for, and other factors, such as how often the vehicle is parked in a garage or enclosed area.

Vinyl Wrap Uses and Applications

Vinyl wraps are used in a variety of automotive applications. The most common uses are exterior color changes, graphics, and business advertising. However, other applications exist for a vinyl wrap, such as interior parts, emblems, and wheels.

The best surface for a long-lasting vinyl wrap application is a flat, non-porous surface that is made of metal or glass. Certain plastics will also work with vinyl wrap if they are free of waxes and chemical agents that are common in interior detailing products. While vinyl wrap is a malleable material that can bend, stretch, and adapt to a variety of curved surfaces (bumpers, door handles, and side mirrors), it takes a certain amount of skill and patience to get the product to lay flat over a curved surface without bubbles, wrinkles, and tears.

If this is your first time working with vinyl-wrap materials, start with one of the more common applications to get a feel for working with the product. The following are seven of the most common vinyl wrap applications.

Complete Color Changes

A complete color change is exactly what it sounds like: chang-

---

This Mercedes-Benz is wrapped in 3M 1080 Satin Canyon Copper.

This Audi is wrapped in 3M 1080 Satin Smoldering Red. The nice thing about satin is that it provides a half-gloss and half-matte look. Satin is truly the new custom look.

One of the questions that we receive most when it comes to wrapping vehicles involves doorjambs. They don't need to be wrapped. We advise our clients to first let us wrap the car, and if they don't like how it looks, we can charge extra and wrap the doorjambs. As you can see, they won't show at all when the doors are closed if you make the lines clean enough.

ing the color of a car, truck, SUV, or motorcycle from its factory paint color to a brand-new color. The process involves covering the entire colored exterior surface of the vehicle with a layer of vinyl wrap. A color-change vinyl-wrap project is one of the most labor-intensive and rewarding projects that you can do for your vehicle. It will transform the look of a vehicle in a matter of days.

Color-change vehicle wraps are not one-size-fits-all projects. There are varying levels that depend on how detailed and complete you want the final product to be. A showroom-quality color change involves removing all exterior trim pieces, including pieces such as door handles, mirrors, emblems, spoilers, etc. It also requires taking the extra time to wrap inner door sills and crevasses around parts, including the trunk and hood. While this adds to the complexity and time required for the color-change project, it provides a professional, finished prod-uct. Depending on your goals for the project, you may choose to only wrap the most visible exterior pieces.

Advantages

The advantages of a color-change vinyl wrap are that the entire painted surface of the vehicle is protected with a layer of 3- to 4- mil vinyl, the vehicle's exterior will look like it just rolled off the assembly line, and you can choose a variety of colors and patterns that are either cost prohib-itive or simply unavailable with tra-ditional paint.

Another benefit of color-change wraps is that if the vehicle is ever damaged, you can simply rewrap the replaced panels of the vehicle without the need for complex paint matching or a respray paint job of the vehicle's entire surface.

Disadvantages

The downsides of a color-change vinyl wrap are the complexity, cost, and time required for the project. A showroom-quality result for this type of wrap can take over 40 hours for even the most experienced and talented vinyl-wrap professionals. If you're working on a large vehicle (a truck, large SUV, or van) the time required can be extensive, and it may require more materials. Later in this book, the process to estimate the time and materials that are needed is addressed.

Partial Wraps

Partial vinyl wraps are one of the easier projects to tackle, especially if this is your first time working with the materials. Partial wraps involve covering only a portion of the vehi-cle, such as the hood, roof, or trunk, with vinyl materials. They do an excellent job of adding contrast to

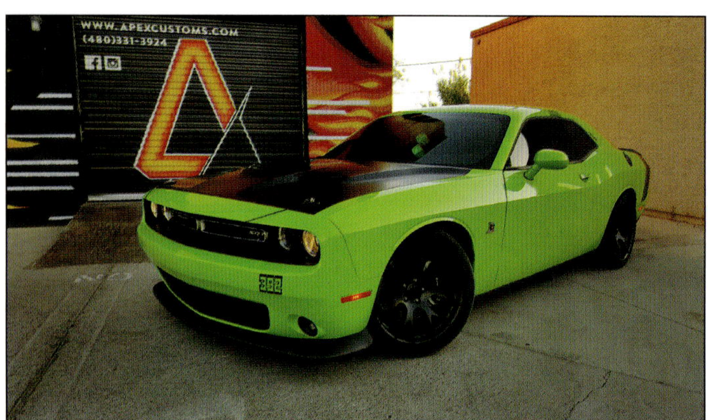

This Dodge Challenger received a 3M 1080 Satin Black hood wrap, rear trunk stripe, and 392 in the front. The trunk stripe and 392 both required use of the plotter. The car was measured, and the graphics were created with the software system for plot and later installed.

Here's a Ford Mustang with 3M 1080 Gloss Silver with Gloss Silver Tron kit. These items are all plotted to the vehicle. The Tron kits are 1-inch lines placed mostly at creases in the vehicle's design. The front stripes are 1 inch wide with 1/2-inch spacing.

the vehicle's exterior appearance. Examples of common partial wraps include adding a gloss black roof to a white SUV or a carbon-fiber appearance to the hood of your gloss-black car.

Advantages

The advantages of partial wraps include using less material, making them cheaper. Partial wraps are generally less complex and easier to complete, and they can be completed faster than a complete vehicle wrap. Partial wraps are also generally easier for the first-time wrapper because they are applied to large surface areas without complex curves. Wrapping the surface area of a car's hood takes less time and is less challenging than a bumper with wide, continuously curved surfaces.

Disadvantages

The most significant downside of a partial wrap is that only a portion of the vehicle's surface is covered. Partial wraps leave the rest of the vehicle's paint surface exposed to weather elements and road debris, which limits the paint protection

benefits of vinyl wrap. Additionally, because you are covering a portion of the vehicle's paint with vinyl, the non-wrapped surfaces of the paint will weather and fade at a different rate than the wrapped surfaces. Because the wrapped surface has a protective layer of vinyl, the paint won't fade as quickly from the sun and won't pick up the same amount of scratches and dings as the non-wrapped surfaces will. When the vinyl is removed a few years down the line, there will be two vastly different colored surfaces, which may decrease the value of the vehicle and damage its visual appearance.

Another downside of a partial wrap is color matching. While partial wraps are good at adding contrast, such as a black roof on a white car, they are not as effective at matching the vehicle's existing paint job. Matching a vinyl-wrap color to the existing factory paint is extremely challenging. If you're considering a partial wrap as a way to color match, such as covering a newly replaced hood to match your existing paint, you most likely will not be satisfied with the result.

Stripe Kits

Stripe kits are one of the more traditional applications of vinyl wrap. Stripe kits have been around for many years, are traditionally seen on race cars, and are a great way to add a sporty look to a vehicle. Vinyl stripe kits can involve laying a strip of vinyl material from one end of the bumper to the other end. They come in a variety of styles, such as a double stripe, single stripe, or even a thick stripe with a smaller pinstripe. The options for a stripe kit are endless and limited only by your creativity.

Stripe kits are available as precut, ready-to-install kits, or a custom kit can be cut by a vinyl-wrap supplier or printer. While in theory, you could cut the stripes out of a roll of vinyl by hand, the best method for creating a kit is to have them cut on a professional plotting machine.

Plotting machines use special software that takes the measurements of the vehicle and calculates the exact dimensions that are needed for the material. Once the software loads the dimensions into the machine, the plotter will make a perfect cut down

The 3M IJ180 custom-printed green with a 3M Sheer Luck Green stripe and Tron *kit were applied to this Mustang. The film base was specialty printed on a large-format HP printer to get the exact color the customer specified. The laminate is gloss.*

Here's a Tesla Model X with a full de-chrome in 3M 1080 Satin Black. The de-chroming on this Tesla includes badges, mirror pivots, the window trim, door handles, and the front grille. We advise the use of powder coating over wrap for wheels, such as these powder coated satin black wheels.

to a fraction of an inch from a large roll of vinyl.

Advantages

The main benefit of stripe kits is that they are generally more affordable and easier to find as premade kits for a wide range of common sports cars. In comparison to a full vehicle wrap, they are also easier and faster to apply because there is a small amount of material to install. Stripe kits are also effective at changing the look of the vehicle by adding contrast and a style that is immediately recognizable by all motorists.

Disadvantages

There are a few downsides of stripe kits to consider before installing one. First, similar to a partial wrap, only a portion of the vehicle is covered. Striped kits will leave the rest of the vehicle's paint surfaces exposed to weather elements and road debris. There is a risk of the paint underneath the stripe kit fading at a different rate than the rest of the vehicle. When the stripe kit is removed, there will be an obvious color contrast that leaves an appear-

ance of less faded paint in the areas where the stripes used to be.

Another downside is that stripe kits take skill to install properly. While you are installing less material on relatively flat, straight surfaces, there is the added challenge of ensuring the stripes line up properly and run straight with the centerline of the vehicle. Most stripes will begin at the bottom of the front bumper, run over the hood, down the roof, over the trunk, and end at the bottom of the rear bumper. It will take a lot of patience, measuring, remeasuring, and aligning the vinyl to ensure that the stripes aren't crooked.

De-Chrome

De-chrome has become one of the most popular applications of vinyl wrap. For some, the look of chrome trim, mirrors, and door handles is a symbol of style and class. For others, all that chrome is simply an eyesore that must go. De-chrome vinyl applications involve covering all of the chrome pieces on the vehicle with vinyl material. While any color or pattern of vinyl can be used for this process, the most common is to use

a gloss or matte black, which is generally referred to as a black-out. The most common parts covered in a de-chrome are trim around the front and rear side windows, trim flashing, accent strips, side mirrors, and door handles.

Advantages

Using vinyl wrap to de-chrome a vehicle has become extremely popular due to the cost and time involved to install vinyl versus pulling the trim pieces and having them professionally scuffed and painted.

For the do-it-yourselfer (DIYer), the chrome paint and plating used by a vehicle manufacturer is extremely difficult to paint with a standard spray can from the automotive store. Even if you take the time and effort to thoroughly prep your trim pieces before painting them, the durability of paint in this application generally does not hold up to the harsh elements to which the exterior trim will be exposed. On top of that, once the pieces are painted, there is no way to go back to the original chrome look if you ever decide to sell or trade in the vehicle. Vinyl wrap, on the other

This Escalade's de-chrome used 3M 1080 Satin Black. Escalades come with many chrome components. As you can see, nearly all the chrome has been wrapped. Powder coating was used to do all but the chrome inserts of the wheels The lights have been tinted with paint. Although, there are films on the market that can be used instead of paint. We use paint as an option and like it better than film in most cases, but that doesn't mean a wrap can't look great.

hand, is simply removed by pulling it off, which can be completed in an afternoon.

A properly installed de-chrome kit can be one of the most satisfying projects that can be done. Benefits include relatively low material cost, ease of installation, and instant gratification as that flashy chrome is covered. As long as you're comfortable with driving with partial chrome still exposed, it's a project that can be done in steps. One weekend, the mirrors can be covered; the next weekend, the window trim can be done.

The most significant benefit of a de-chrome project is that the original OEM chrome parts aren't damaged by sanding and painting. De-chrome allows the vehicle to return to its stock look if the vehicle is ever sold or traded in.

For some vehicles, you can purchase OEM replacement parts in colors other than chrome and replace the chrome parts. While this is the most reliable and preferred approach to de-chroming a vehicle, the cost and labor involved with this approach is generally prohibitive.

Disadvantages

Using vinyl to de-chrome has some potential drawbacks. First, a vinyl wrap is susceptible to rock chips and harsh weather. While vinyl has far more durability than other de-chrome methods, such as rubberized paint, over time the vinyl will chip and peel. Another potential challenge with vinyl wrapping trim pieces is how the vehicle's trim is often surrounded by rubber seals to prevent moisture and air from entering the cabin of the vehicle. While there are installation methods to help cope with these obstacles that are covered later in the book, the proximity of rubber pieces to the trim can make a de-chrome installation more challenging.

Interior Parts

Vinyl wrapping the interior of a vehicle is less common than vinyl wrapping the exterior but is another potential application that is often overlooked. The most common reason to use vinyl on an interior part is to change the color or texture of the dash, door, and center console trim pieces. Vinyl patterns, such as carbon fiber, brushed steel, or a solid color with a matte finish, are excellent ways to spruce up the interior appearance of a vehicle.

While the interior parts are not exposed to the same harsh elements as a bumper or hood, the protective benefits that vinyl wrap provides are also beneficial. Vinyl will protect the interior from the sun's ultraviolet (UV) rays as well as scratches and scuffs from passengers.

Not all interior pieces are good candidates for a vinyl wrap. Fabrics and certain plastics simply do not have the adhesion properties that are required. Common interior cleaning and protective products can also cause issues with the vinyl adhering properly and affect the longevity of the vinyl. Additionally, many interior pieces have complex shapes and curves, which makes installation extremely challenging.

Advantages

The two main benefits of using vinyl wrap in an interior application are the low cost and the protective properties of the material. The material required to wrap the small interior pieces is minimal. There are even suppliers on the market that sell precut vinyl kits for certain vehicle applications to make installation a breeze. A vinyl wrap provides an effective way to keep parts prone to wear and tear relatively safe from damage. They help maintain your vehicle's resale value and keep the surface underneath looking as good as the day the vinyl was installed.

Disadvantages

The biggest downside of using vinyl in an interior application is the complexity of installation. Vinyl wraps are best utilized on large flat surfaces. Interior parts are often small and complex in shape and contour, which makes the installation of vinyl challenging. Small parts are prone to wrinkles, bubbles, and lifting edges due to how it is difficult to get the proper stretch and adhesion for a reliable application.

Graphics

Graphics are one of the most widely used applications of vinyl wrap. The most common vinyl graphics are cut in predesigned shapes and patterns using industrial plotting machines. Then, they are sold and ready to apply.

This is a 3M 1080 Deep Matte Black full wrap with 3M 1080 Gloss White, a Satin Smoldering Red center stripe, and plotted 3M 1080 Deep Matte Black buckeye decals.

If you've ever purchased a decal to stick on a bumper or windshield, you've most likely had experience with a vinyl graphic. Common applications of vinyl graphics include logos, mascots, abstract designs, and lettering. While the most widely utilized graphics are relatively small in size, vinyl graphics also come in sizes large enough to cover an entire vehicle. In addition to precut graphics, a commercial print shop can design and cut just about any vinyl graphic.

Vinyl graphics are an excellent way to accent the exterior of your vehicle. They can be applied directly to your vehicle's paint surface, on top of vinyl wrap, or underneath a vinyl wrap for a ghosted appearance. Graphics are cut from standard vinyl-wrap material, so the color, texture, and pattern options are as expansive as any other vinyl application. The installation and removal methods for vinyl graphics are generally the same as any other vinyl-wrap application.

Advantages

The advantages of vinyl graphics are their low cost, ease of installation, and unique ability to add a touch of personal style to a vehicle. Precut vinyl graphics are often manufactured in large volumes to make them affordable to even the lowest-budget project. Large and custom-designed graphics carry a higher price but remain considerably cheaper than alternatives, such as airbrushed graphics.

While it is time consuming to install a vinyl graphic properly and ensure that it is straight and the adhesive of the graphic bonds well to the vehicle, the process is still considerably quicker than other vinyl applications. Best of all, vinyl graphics are easy to remove, and when cut out of a quality vinyl material, they will rarely leave glue residue behind unlike their sticker counterparts.

Disadvantages

The key downside of a vinyl graphic is its durability. In general, when a part or surface is covered with vinyl, the edges of the vinyl are wrapped or tucked around the part. This process prevents the vinyl from lifting or peeling off the surface. In most cases, vinyl graphics have sharp, exposed edges that provide the outline for the graphic. These exposed edges are prone to peeling and lifting and are susceptible to things, such as car wash brushes, ice scrapers, windows rolling up and down, etc.

Finally, as with vinyl racing stripes and partial wraps, the paint surface beneath a vinyl graphic will fade and weather at a different rate than painted surfaces, so vinyl graphics run the risk of leaving a permanent mark on a vehicle's factory paint in the shape of the graphic.

Business Wraps

Business wraps are the most widely recognized application of vinyl wrap. Similar to color-change and partial wraps, they cover large sections or the entirety of the vehicle in vinyl material. The difference between a business wrap and a color-change wrap is that business wraps use a different style of vinyl material and contain printed advertising for a business, charity, or event. The vinyl material used for a business wrap has a unique surface that allows large-format printers to print custom colors and designs. Printable vinyl comes in a variety of styles, including standard, reflective, perforated, transparent, and translucent. Generally, these vinyl materials require a special over-laminate to be applied on top of the printed surface to protect the printed ink from the elements.

Business wraps come in a wide range of sizes, styles, and applications. Common examples include display advertising across the side of a bus, a work van for your local plumber, a food truck with a graphic that displays delicious grilled cheese, or your neighbor's pickup truck with a logo and phone number. A business wrap can be a full-vehicle or partial wrap, or it can even be just a vinyl graphic with a phone number.

The benefits of business wraps are that they are a cost-effective and an efficient method for advertising. They are essentially a rolling billboard that receives thousands of visual impressions. They also have the added benefit of protecting the vehicle's original paint surface. Business graphic vinyl wraps help protect a business's investment by maintaining resale value for the work vehicle.

Additionally, because a business wrap can be printed from any design, it is an effective way to create a truly unique and eye-catching design for a vehicle.

The most significant drawback of a business wrap is the cost and labor associated. Unlike a color-change wrap, a business wrap has the added expense of custom design, printing, and laminating.

Additionally, business wraps are more tedious to install because the panels must be aligned to create a seamless visual effect between seams, and if one of the printed panels is screwed up, additional vinyl materials and printing are required.

A 3M IJ180 full print wrap is on the Rolling Stones' trailer. When large clients want work done, they generally have their own designers create the design. However, unless a vehicle wrap expert is hired, it can be difficult for the other designer to understand vehicle wrap formatting, which is simply sizing the picture that you see on the screen to the realness of the vehicle's size. It's also important to understand how to place graphics.

This picture is of a vehicle after graphic design and undergoing paneling. Vehicles can be paneled many different ways. Obviously, the film is only as large as a printer, which is not as large as a car, so sections of the wrap are printed and built when applied. Hide any panel transitions in the vehicle's panels or where the body areas end and begin, such as a door or a fender. The graphic also needs to flow. An important part of a graphic should not end up on a door handle. Paneling is an art.

A 3M 1080 Matte Purple with matte silver plotted decals and 3M IJ180 custom fade prints is shown. It is possible to use a combination of many materials to make one amazing result. Since this client wanted the fade in the side letters, the only way to do this is print.

Business wraps require specialized software, printing equipment, and installation skills and are generally best left to the professionals.

Vinyl Wrap Benefits

The primary reason that automotive enthusiasts consider vinyl wrapping is to change the appearance of a vehicle. The wide variety of color choices, unique patterns, and textures are often enough to convince a person to invest in a color change wrap.

However, there are several additional benefits offered by vinyl wrap that make it a superior automotive restyling product. Let's take a look at the top five reasons to consider vinyl wrap for your next project.

Paint Protection

Unlike traditional paint, a vinyl wrap adds a layer of protection to the vehicle's surface. Any time the vehicle is on the road, its paint is exposed to several hazards. Rock chips, road debris, bugs, tree sap, and salt have the potential to cause serious damage. Similar to paint protection films, such as Clear Bra, vinyl wrap provides a protective polymer layer 3 to 4 mil thick between the surface of the vehicle's paint and the inevitable road hazard.

In addition to the protective layer, the PVC polymer layer has flexible shock-absorbing properties that reduce the impact of objects that strike the vehicle's surface.

Vinyl wraps can be washed similarly to OEM paint. Although, our rule of thumb is to treat it like a gloss-black paint job. You wouldn't take a gloss black paint though a brush-based car wash. You would be careful with the type of cloths and equipment used to wash the car. It is fine to use a pressure washer, and you can never go wrong a with good old hand wash.

Reversible

One of the most important benefits of a vinyl wrap is how easily it is removed. The adhesives in modern vinyl wrap have been uniquely designed to allow for easy removal without damaging the paint underneath. It's entirely reversible, which makes it a viable solution for just about any automotive application.

If you lease a vehicle, it can be vinyl wrapped without causing permanent damage to the expensive paint job. If you want to change the color or style of your vehicle every six months, pull the old vinyl and install new vinyl. If the car is going to be sold or traded in, pull the vinyl to make it more desirable for the average car buyer.

The reason to use top-quality vinyl and remove it within its life span is simple. Quality vinyl wrap is removed in a few hours. When the film gets old, it starts to separate from its adhesive layer, which leaves it all over the paint. Within the right time span, this happens less often and involves almost no adhesive remover. This topic is addressed in greater detail later in the book. The key insights are as follows: don't be fooled that all wrap films are the same, and remove the wrap within its proper time frame.

Cost

Changing the color and style of a vehicle can turn into a expensive project. Quality automotive paint jobs start in the $10,000 range and go up significantly from there.

Vinyl wrap, on the other hand, is generally a quarter to a third of that price. If you're willing to put in the labor, the only true cost is for materials, which can drop the cost to less than $1,000. Not only is vinyl wrap more affordable than traditional paint but it also provides a better return on investment than other paint alternatives. Paint alternatives, such as rubberized paint, may be initially slightly cheaper, but they have a far shorter life span.

Versatility

Vinyl wrap is a versatile product that is applied to a variety of surfaces, both interior and exterior. Metal, glass, and plastic are all viable candidates for vinyl-wrap applications. It can be installed on exterior parts that are exposed to rain, sleet, snow, and dirt, as well as interior parts that are exposed to cleaning chemicals and accidental spills.

Uniqueness

The most exciting benefit to vinyl wrap is its unique factor. Vinyl wrap is available in a variety of unique colors, patterns, and finishes that no other paint or paint alternative project can offer. While matte finishes are available with traditional paint, they require a considerable amount of care and maintenance to retain the finish. A matte vinyl wrap, on the other hand, is installed, treated, and maintained in the same manner as other finishes.

Vinyl wrap is also available in custom patterns, such as carbon fiber, brushed steel, brushed titanium, metallics, camo, and neon. Recently, vinyl wrap suppliers have released color-shifting and color-changing vinyl that changes color depending on the angle on which it is viewed.

What Works Well with Vinyl Wrap

Vinyl wrap is a highly versatile product that offers a wide array of possible applications. While vinyl wrap is a versatile and dynamic product, there are some applications that work best as well as some that you should avoid.

Flat Surfaces

The best possible application for a vinyl-wrap installation is a relatively flat, smooth, and nonporous surface that has been cleaned of any waxes or contaminants. Door and body panels, large trim pieces, hoods, roofs, trunks, spoilers, and smooth interior panels all make for ideal vinyl wrap applications. The large exterior panels of a vehicle make an ideal canvas for vinyl-wrap application and allow large, smooth, nonporous surface areas of adhesive contact, tucked

An Apex Customs Porsche is shown in PPG red/orange paint with a gloss black painted roof. Although a wrap can be made to look like this, it is actually paint. This is a Porsche we built. You will never be able to tell the difference between a wrap and paint in photos. If the paint or wrap is done well, it can be difficult to tell in person too.

It takes a tremendous amount of prep and time to get a vehicle ready for paint. Here, our painter is preparing to paint the firewall on this F-100. In this case, wrap is not suitable for the firewall.

edges for strain anchoring, and large sweeping angles and curves for continuous and gradual stretch.

The worst possible application for vinyl wrap contains porous surfaces, has complex curves and shapes, and is subject to contaminants, such as wax, petrochemicals, solvents, dirt, and dust particles. Avoid parts that are subject to extreme weather and require regular flex and movement. Examples include wood, textured plastics, rubber gaskets, rusted metals, tires, leather and upholstery vinyl, and suspension components.

With the right installation techniques, such as using heat for stretch-ing and shrinking, a vinyl wrap can be installed on a number of complex shapes, contours, and ridges. However, complex shapes, such as a side mirror, require special skill and patience to massage the material into shape. There is always risk involved with complex shapes, deep ridges, and sharp corners that the adhesive of the vinyl will release or that the vinyl will expand or shrink and cause edges to lift and release.

Many plastic and rubber components on a vehicle use petrochemical solvents in the products themselves or are used in molds when the product is manufactured. For example, a plastic door panel may have a thin layer of chemicals or wax on the surface that will prevent the adhesives on the vinyl wrap from properly adhering. Many plastic trim and interior pieces have rough, porous surfaces that have the same effect of preventing the vinyl adhesives from forming a solid bond.

Vinyl Wrap versus Paint

Since the early days of automobiles, paint has been the go-to source to add color and style to your ride. It's time tested and proven to be a reliable coating for automotive applications, so why would you consider vinyl wrap over paint? While paint is the standard in OEM automotive coatings and aftermarket restyling, there are several advantages to vinyl wrap that should be considered when you plan your next project.

Time and Expense

The first and most important benefit to consider is time and expense. While there are paint service companies that will offer a $500 special on an old jalopy, a quality and lasting automotive paint job is an extremely time-consuming and expensive project.

Costs for a decent paint job can range from $10,000 to $50,000. They require hundreds of working hours and highly skilled technicians to produce a professional finished product. Painting requires a significant amount of prep work. In many cases, a vehicle must be sanded all the way down to its bare metal, prepped, primed, sanded, sprayed, clear coated, wet sanded, buffed, and polished. That's not even taking into account the imperfections from the dust that may land in your wet paint halfway

Although Plasti Dip may look similar to matte black vinyl wraps, it leaves several things to be desired. The material is extremely prone to chemical reversal. Gasoline, for example, will almost immediately ruin the product.

through the process, which would force you to start all over again.

Tools and Skills

Automotive painting projects require specialized tools and skills to get the job done right: sanding tools, special paint mixing equipment, spray guns, air compressors, filtration, and, most importantly, a paint booth. While it is possible to get decent results in the garage on a small trim piece or engine cover with a rattle can, the results are most likely going to be subpar on any large components. Even the most experienced painters with the right equipment run into issues with achieving high-quality, eye-catching results.

Paint is also a permanent solution. Once you've applied automotive paint to the surface of the vehicle, there is no going back without sanding and starting over. Painting is not an option if you're looking for a color change on a leased car. Aftermarket paint jobs often reduce the resale value of a vehicle because future owners don't know if the job was completed correctly. Poor paint jobs can lead to rust that can eat

away the vehicle's skeleton from the inside out.

By contrast, a properly installed vinyl wrap can look just as good as OEM paint without all of the risk and expense. Vinyl wraps are significantly cheaper, and any automotive enthusiast can install them in a garage with a few cheap tools. Best of all, the product is completely reversible so if you screw up the installation, need to turn your lease back in to the dealer, or want to change colors again, pull the vinyl in an afternoon, and you're back to where you started. Finally, vinyl wrap offers the vehicle's paint a level of protection from the elements, UV rays, and road debris. If a rock hits the bumper and damages the vinyl, simply pull the vinyl and rewrap.

Vinyl Wrap versus Paint Alternatives

When planning an automotive restyling project, it's important to understand all the products available so that you can choose the best product for the project. It is always important to utilize the right tool for the

These powder-coated blue Jeep components are under the vehicle, and the springs require some range of motion. Powder coating is a better product for areas of potential high impact and movement. Many of these items are near impossible to wrap. Wrap doesn't need to solve every problem, but neither does powder coating. Powder coating is not easily removed.

You can wrap a wheel, but powder coating does a much better job. The moment a full wheel like this is hit by a rock, it will pierce the film and show what's underneath. Wrap for wheels is better used as an accent. Wheels can be wrapped, but if the goal is satin black, powder coating is the better option.

Powder coating requires much more equipment (large ovens and expensive application guns) than vinyl wrap.

job, and vinyl wrap has healthy competition in the automotive restyling market these days. Powder coating, bed liner, and liquid wrap are all traditional paint alternative products to consider for a project. Each of these products has its place in automotive restyling, so let's take a look at how each compares to vinyl wrap.

Vinyl Wrap versus Powder Coating

Powder coating uses a process called electrostatic spray deposition (ESD) to apply powder using an electrostatic charge to a metal substrate. Before the powder is applied, the metal substrate is chemically treated and then sandblasted to create an etched surface. After the metal surface is prepped, the metal is grounded, and powder is applied using a specialized applicator gun that applies the electrostatic charge to the powder particles. The powder particles are attracted to the grounded metal surface, which results in a smooth, even surface. Once the powder is applied, the coated metal is placed into a curing oven, where the powder is chemically transformed into a durable coating.

Powder coating is an extremely durable coating because of the long chain molecules created during the process, which results in a high cross-link density within the coating. It provides an attractive finish that is resistant to extreme weather, certain chemicals, moisture, and ultraviolet light.

Powder coating is most popular in the automotive world for restyling wheels due to its durability against road debris, weather elements, and brake dust. Powder coating is often used for the factory OEM coating on the majority of factory and aftermarket wheels. It is also an excellent product for solid metal parts in any automotive application that is subject to extreme temperatures and prone to high impact, such as the engine bay, suspension components, and truck and SUV bumpers.

Powder Coating Rubber and Plastic

While powder coating is an excellent product for high-impact areas and solid metal components that are prone to extreme heat, it is not suitable for any components made of plastic or rubber due to the high curing temperatures required.

Additionally, powder coating requires each component to be chemically stripped, sandblasted, electrically grounded, powder applied, and baked in an oven under extreme temperatures, which makes it a poor choice both economically and practically for body panels. Vinyl wrap is the superior product and choice for rubber and plastic components as well as large surface body panels.

Plasti Dip can look similar to a full vinyl wrap, but there are several downsides, including immediate reversal of the product if exposed to gasoline. Gas is not good for vinyl wrap if left on the surface for an extended period, but it will not immediately reverse the product.

Vinyl Wrapping High-Heat Areas

In comparison, a vinyl wrap is a poor choice for high-impact areas and components that are subject to extreme heat. Vinyl wrap expands and contracts with heat. This expansion and contraction causes vinyl wrap to lose its shape and adhesion to the surface to which it is applied. In extreme temperature situations, a vinyl wrap will melt away. Vinyl wrap is also a relatively thin material that will rip and puncture under high-impact situations that you might expect to see on a suspension component or truck bumper.

Vinyl Wrap versus Liquid Wrap

Liquid wrap is a relatively new product to the automotive restyling industry that has gained considerable popularity in recent years. In comparison to painting and other paint alternatives, a liquid wrap is generally the most affordable option for any color change or coating project.

At its core, a liquid wrap is an air-dry, specialty rubber coating that can be applied to a wide range of surfaces. It can be removed by peeling off the coating once it has been cured. It is a flexible coating with insulating properties and some dura-

bility. Many manufacturers produce variants of liquid wrap, including AutoFlex, Raail, and Halo EFX, but none are as well-known as Plasti Dip.

Liquid Wrap Advantages

Liquid wrap has several benefits in automotive applications. It is affordable, widely available, relatively easy to use, can be applied to a range of surfaces, and generally does not require the same level of preparation as paint, vinyl wrap, powder coating, and bed liners. It also provides some protection of the surface underneath the coating. For the DIY enthusiast, it can be a great product for covering small components, such as a vehicle emblem or trim piece.

Liquid Wrap Disadvantages

Liquid wrap has several drawbacks that do not make it a viable product for most automotive applications. Overall, the product is not durable. For example, most enthusiasts find that after covering any exterior

It's not easy to see the difference between paint, a wrap, and Plasti Dip in a photo. Plasti Dip, if applied right, can have a similar touch and feel to vinyl wrap. Certain Plasti Dip–like products are made of the same basic polymeric structures as the vinyl that is used in this book. Liquid forms, however, can be chemically reversed easily by exposure to common chemicals, such as gasoline and tire shine.

component, such as wheels or a front bumper grille, the rubber coating starts to peel and chip in a short time. Most applications won't last more than a few months before chips from stones and road debris begin to cause imperfections in the coated surface.

The product also tends to perform poorly with chemical resistance, UV protection, and foreign substrates, such as bird droppings. Many common products with which a vehicle will come into contact, such as tire-shine chemicals and gasoline, will quickly damage and remove the product altogether in some cases. Even basic cleaning techniques, such as hand scrubbing, can quickly ruin your liquid-wrap coating.

Compared to vinyl wrap, a liquid wrap is more difficult to remove. Unless the liquid-wrap material was applied in thick coats, it can be challenging to pull more than one tiny piece at a time during removal. When the product is difficult to remove, there is a risk of causing significant damage to the vehicle's paint surface during the process.

In many cases, liquid vinyl is sprayed directly onto the vehicle. This causes the product to be applied in areas in which it was not intended, such as seams and crevasses, which makes removal nearly impossible.

Liquid wrap also has a shorter life span than vinyl wrap. Most liquid wrap coatings begin to break down within two to three years, whereas vinyl wrap can last up to seven years.

Vinyl Wrap versus Bed Liner

Bed liner is a product that, until recently, was used primarily to protect the metal bed of trucks. It is a highly durable product that has been

Permanent sprayable bedliners have been used on all sorts of exterior vehicle applications. We are thrilled to have the wrap lookalike version. This Avery Rugged Bedrock Grey is the bedliner lookalike, but it is 100-percent reversible.

available for many years.

In recent years, the product has become popular in many automotive applications beyond truck beds. The seemingly indestructible properties of bed liner make it an excellent application for nearly any automotive part that is exposed to high impact.

The most common application of bed liner is on off-road vehicles that are exposed to hazards to paint, such as tree branches, mud, and rocks. Many off-road Jeep, truck, and SUV owners cover the entire exterior of the vehicle in bed liner, including body panels, bumpers, running boards, roll cages, etc. Bed liner is a versatile product that can be applied to a variety of metals and plastics.

Bed liner has a few downsides. Most importantly, it is permanent. Once you have applied bed liner to a part, the only way to remove it is through sanding, grinding, chiseling, and using harsh chemicals. The removal of bed liner will cause significant damage to the painted surface underneath. Another drawback is that while some bed liner prod-

This is a close-up of the Avery rugged material. The texture is reflecting the sun on the hood panel. The rough texture can be felt when it is touched.

ucts can be colored in almost any OEM color, the unique patterns and color effects that are offered by vinyl wrap are not matched. Bed liner is textured, so if you're looking for a smooth, shiny surface on your vehicle, bed liner is not for you.

While some manufacturers offer bed liner in sprayable rattle cans, true bed liner products require expensive specialized equipment to apply. Unlike a vinyl wrap that can produce showroom results in your garage, bed liner requires professional expertise and equipment to produce a quality lasting result.

Vinyl Wrap Science and Characteristics

The 1080 Gloss Black accents look amazing on this 3M 1080 Satin Dark Grey Tesla full wrap.

This BMW is wrapped in Satin Perfect Blue 3M 1080 with Gloss Black 3M 1080 accents, including the roof. A gloss black roof is a great way to add some class to the vehicle. It gives the appearance of a panoramic roof.

There is no reason to get into a full chemistry lesson on vinyl and its chemical composition. It is not relevant to learn how to install vinyl onto a vehicle. However, knowledge about the film can provide a greater understanding to installation procedures, and it can help troubleshoot problems.

Science

A film is a form of polymer, and in the case of vinyl wrap, it is a vinyl polymer. Poly means "many" or "repeatable." When chemical bonds are formed and repeat, they form a polymer. The stronger the repeatable bond structure, the stronger the item will be.

Many people know the chemical formula for water: H_2O. It consists of two hydrogen atoms and one oxygen atom that bond together to become water. Now, think a bit grander. Think of a strong bond, but now it also repeats like links in a chain. The strength of the film has a lot to do with its composition. The films that we most commonly use are polyvinyl chloride (PVC). Although they are not perfect, they currently have an edge over the others for durability, outdoor longevity, and versatility.

This bus decal was made with calendared film. Calendared films are much cheaper than cast films, so they are generally used for flat-panel advertisements, such as the one.

Avery offers this color called Supreme Satin Orange. One of the hardest parts of a wrap is getting the bumpers just right.

Types

Cast and calendared are the various types of production in which vinyl film is made. The production process has ties to the quality that you can expect to receive. The way a film is produced has an impact on the overall quality of the product as well as its cost. Note that there are tremendous advances every day. The advances continue to close the gap between the quality of these processes.

Calendared Film

Simply put, calendared film is for flat-panel, short-term applications. The rule of thumb is to generally stay away from anything calendared for high-end automotive application. These films won't conform or perform the same way in the long term. The production process is like that of cast films, except it is extruded via rollers and formed at much lower temperatures. This makes it harder to get thinner and more conformable films. The extrusion process subjects the film to immense pressure that can cause increased shrinkage tendencies later.

Cast Films

This book's purpose is to teach you how to wrap high-end vehicles. For this purpose, the only films worth speaking about are cast. Formed at much higher temperatures than calendared film, this film is placed into a mold to be cast into a better film. Think of it as mixing a giant bowl of polymers, spreading them on a cookie sheet, and baking them in the oven. This is how cast films are made.

Adhesives and Activation

Quality vinyl wrap has super sophisticated adhesive technology. It is made to react to heat and easily release once activated. Once it is back to normal temperature, the adhesive once again bonds and becomes solid. It is possible to peel up the wrap without first heating it, but it is much harder. Heating the film will also allow the film to better conform

This is a full Jeep wrap in Matte Deep Black. It is possible to wrap parts such as hinges, but it's a better idea to buy a set of plastic covers to make it more durable in the long term.

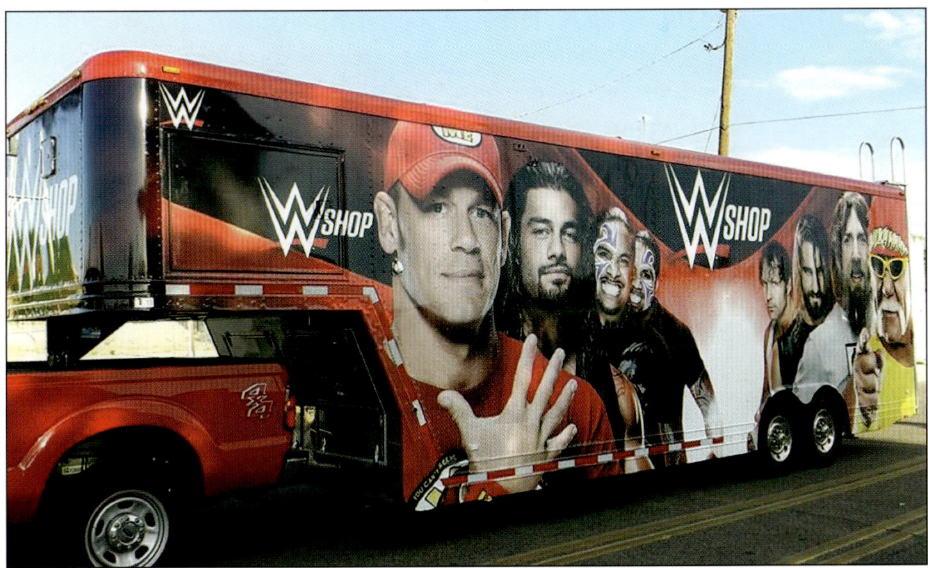

Many pieces of vinyl were used to create this WWE custom-printed trailer with 3M IJ180.

Air Channels and Bubbles

Here's a simple science lesson: Air is comprised of molecules. Heat excites those molecules and causes them to bounce around. It is this bouncing of molecules that causes bubbles. Later, when panel installation is covered, we will discuss how to avoid bubbles. There can even be air spread across the film on a panel that has been laid and looks completely flat. When this film gets into the sun, the molecules will excite and cause a bubble where there hadn't been one before. The good news is that after this initial showing of a bubble, it can be pushed out and not reappear. Many people worry about having bubbles down the road, but once the air is expelled, it won't ever naturally get under the film and cause another bubble.

Air channels are like little corridors in the film. They are pathways where the air can be pushed out. If the film is spread across a panel and pushed with a squeegee or your

to the surface. The film will take the shape of whatever it is applied to when treated with heat.

Great films have great adhesives; they will bond and not separate from the film. This is important in an install because you don't want the adhesive layer to leave anything on the panel as you reposition the film. In short, you want the glue to stay with the film and not on the substrate.

Over long periods of time, even good films will separate from their adhesive layer. That is why it is important to remove films within their life span. If the adhesive separates, it can take quite a bit of work to get it off.

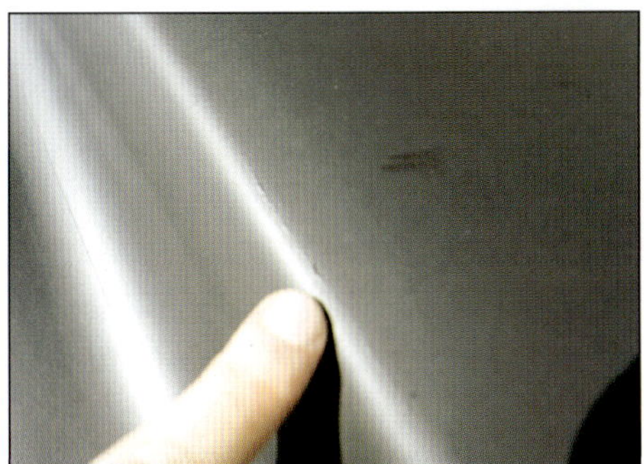

After a wrap is installed, it is important to get the vehicle out in the sun. The sun will excite the air molecules and cause them to find one another and cause a bubble. It is common to have some unseen air lurking to pop up when heat is introduced. Some small bubbles formed here but were easily pressed out of the film.

too many to list here, but we will discuss a few of the more popular ones.

Colors as vast as the rainbow and solids, such as gloss black, satin blue, or matte orange, have become staples in the wrap world.

We've heard many people say, "I would like to wrap my car, but I don't like the matte look."

Matte wrap had become so synonymous with vehicle wrapping that many didn't know it was possible to get anything else.

Gloss Wrap

A gloss wrap will look identical to your gloss OEM paint job. In fact, if you walk into our shop, we like to dare people to try and tell which panel is wrap and which is paint.

hand, it will allow the air to be pushed out of these predesigned little exits. This is yet another feature to a high-quality vinyl film. Having film with air channels allows for a much easier and better install.

Finishes and Patterns

Vinyl wrap has come a long way since the simple advertising decals with which we have become familiar. Once vehicle wrapping became more than just advertisements and evolved into a tool to customize your personal vehicle, the options began to grow by leaps and bounds.

The manufacturers all seek to one-up each other with the next greatest color or finish. This has led to thousands of options. There are

This hoverboard features a Hexis alligator wrap. Yes, there are films in alligator, sequin, and more. They do not tend to conform or last like an exterior-purposed vehicle film, but they can be used in fun applications.

This 3M 1080 gloss black full wrap features a plotted stripe. The Avery Supreme Gloss Pearl White side stripe breaks up this street rod nicely.

This 3M Color Flip Satin Flip Glacial Frost full wrap show-cases hints of purple from various angles under various lighting.

Here is a 3M 1080 Satin White full wrap. We advise our clients to opt for satin white over matte. Matte white can be difficult to maintain and can mark easily. The satin has a slight sheen for protection.

Satin Wrap

A satin wrap is a bit more likely to be exposed as wrap because few manufactures offer a satin paint job. Satin is approximately halfway between matte and gloss. Satin films have a slight silky sheen that is not as brilliant and shiny as gloss.

Matte Wrap

Matte is a dull film with no sheen. Each of these finishes can be ordered in a variety of colors, including some of the more recent color shifts.

Beyond colors and finishes, there are several other popular films. Carbon fibers are readily requested and come in a variety of colors. Brushed films that give the appearance of a metal-type finish are especially popular for wrapping interior trim.

Chrome Wrap

A chrome wrap is the last type of wrap that we will discuss. Have you ever seen a vehicle driving around that looks like a mirror or raw metal

Dueling matte wraps in black and red take some of the shine off the usual factory paint jobs.

Avery's Supreme Blue Chrome is vibrant. Black accents help break up the car and pair well with the blue chrome.

new. The adhesive technology on high-end vinyl is out of this world; it is solid when applied but can be heated and released. Vinyl films have taken over the custom industry and are giving expensive, high-end paint jobs a run for their money.

Appearance

Vinyl films come in large rolls. Once you lay out the roll, unravel it to cut your panels. Films can look textured like brushed or carbon fiber. They come in gloss to mimic the appearance of a high-gloss paint job. They can appear to be dull, such as the appearance of a matte film. They also come in satin and have a 50-50 gloss-to-matte finish that leaves just a slight sheen.

Recently, satin films have taken over matte in terms of popularity. Even several manufactures are getting in on satin finishes. The general appearance of films is vast, as manufacturers continue to extend their offerings.

Large rolls of white film can be loaded into a printer and turned into anything your creativity can design. In recent years, people have started to print designs onto just about any film, including chrome.

Several manufacturers make various overlay films. These are films

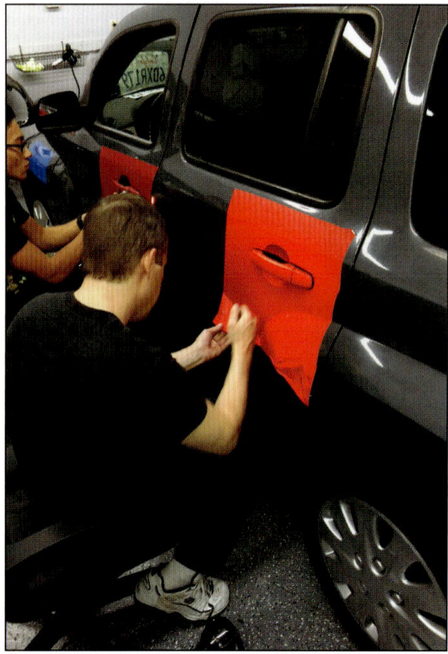

These 3M training facility students apply film to this HHR to practice door-handle and panel laying. We strongly advise removing door handles for a better result. This vehicle has been wrapped hundreds of times and the OEM paint is still undamaged. Good films, such as Avery and 3M, will leave no vehicle damage after wrap removal.

shined up? That is a chrome wrap. These were all the rage not so long ago when money was no option and you really wanted your vehicle to stand out. Now, they are somewhat fading in popularity.

Characteristics

As much as all of us in the industry hate to describe it this way, vinyl is a super sophisticated sticker—but sort of like a sticker on steroids. It can be folded, stomped, beat up, and then heated up and brought back to

A custom hoverboard is wrapped in 3M IJ180 print film. Vinyl wrap can be used on all kinds of items. In the background, see how the pieces of this hoverboard wrap have been plotted and designed to be applied in separate pieces.

This full-vehicle wrap in camo is a custom design with 3M IJ180 film.

can be laminated over another film, so now the options are truly endless. Someone can take a brushed overlay film and add it over a graphically printed image of a sunset or take a carbon-fiber overlay and put it over our ever-famous Joe's Plumbing print.

Longevity

The longevity of the film depends on a variety of things: the environment, the way the owner maintains the film, and even the brand.

The environment has a tremendous impact on how long the film will last. In Arizona, the intense sun is a factor. Many manufacturers cut their life span ratings for a film in half for harsh climates. If you're in state where it snows in the winter, this can also have an impact on the film due to the constant freezing and warming as well as salt from the road, which decreases the film's life span.

In addition, the finish that is chosen and the environment will have an impact on the film. For instance, a matte film in a harsh sun environment will mean a shorter life of the film. Matte film tends to dehydrate faster than products such as satin or gloss. Think of your skin. When you are in the sun, the first thing your skin does is dehydrate, and then it starts to burn. Film does the same thing, but instead of burning, it will begin to fade and then eventually crack.

The more you care for anything, the better it will last, and films are no exception. If a vehicle is wrapped, it should be washed once a week. Contaminants on the film speed up the degradation of the film. Many people live in large cities with heavy pollution, which will attach itself to the film. Combine that with a bit of morning dew, and an acidic chemical reaction happens right on the vehicle. It is important to wash the vehicle once a week.

When all is said and done, most films are rated from one to seven years. Manufacturers rate films for various areas of the country as well as the panel location on the vehicle. A horizontal panel, such as one on your hood, is not expected to last nearly as long as the bottom of a door panel. This is due to the direct sunlight. Specialty films, such as chrome, will not get any life rating from most manufacturers and aren't even guaranteed to last a day. There are films,

If a film is not removed in its life span, it can leave behind a glue residue without proper preheat as seen here. Old film is much more difficult to remove and requires a lot of 3M adhesive remover to get rid of the glue.

mostly in graphics divisions, that are rated for 10 years, but when it comes to custom application films, it is best to do a bit of research as to the manufacturer's rating of the film.

Durability

Two majorly different misconceptions about film are circulating. People either think that it is bombproof and can hold up to any impact or they think it's super fragile. Well, it is neither. It depends on the film in question, but vinyl will not hold up to a rogue shopping cart or a tree branch with a sharp end.

If the door is dinged, it can damage the film, and the car will not be safe from a key and your ex. Rock chips will also damage the film. There are films that are specially designed to prevent rock chips, but color-change films will not hold up the same way. Protection films or a Clear Bra are specifically designed to protect the paint. They are a much thicker mil and harder to conform.

The good news is that the vehicle wrap will protect the paint, but it will be at the expense of the film being damaged. It is the first safety barrier in the protection of your OEM paint. We have seen the crazy ex with a key scenario, and the film takes the beating, yet the paint is perfect after removal.

Film is not fragile, either. It has about the same durability of a paint job. It can stand up to car washes and pressure washers. We have even seen it stand up to a great day of off-roading.

To add extra durability, use ceramic coating products. This will help with durability as well as longevity. They even make it easier to clean.

Vinyl wrap is so versatile that it can be rolled into a ball like this, pulled apart, heated, and flattened back to near perfection. Heating a film can make the film lose the memory of its current shape and transform back to the way it was born: factory flat.

This is after the vinyl wrap ball film was heated and slowly pulled apart. The film will adjust back to its original flat panel shape. With some heat, the wrap will forget just about any position in which it was placed. While it's not ideal for many reasons to roll vinyl wrap into a ball and then place it on a car, it can be done.

Ease of Removal

Film choice has a large impact on many variables. Ease of removal is no exception. Good films are removed rather easily, and bad films may never be removed easily.

For the sake of argument, we will assume that we helped you stay away from a bad film. The wonderful thing about vehicle wraps is they should be 100 percent removable. Since vinyl is heat activated, all that one needs to do is heat the film, find an edge, and slowly start to pull. The longer the film has been on the vehicle, the harder it will be to remove.

If it is long past the removal time, you will be in for quite the week. If you are within the removal time frame, use a bit of elbow grease and a few hours to a day is enough time to fully remove a film. The better the film, the less adhesive that will be left behind. This is important because it will take hours to scrub the adhesive off with a chemical if the residue is left.

For the most part, wrap is easy to remove, and the wonderful thing is that you are back to your OEM paint and ready for another wrap in no time.

Stretch and Shrink

Vinyl wrap film is designed to stretch up to 20 percent of its original size, but it also has a memory that can be jogged with the introduction of heat to bring it back to its original size. This is important because it allows the installer to apply the film to concave surfaces and bends in panels in a much easier fashion.

Myths

After installing thousands of wraps and discussing vinyl with thousands of people, the wrap world is still a mystery to the average person. There are almost two kinds of people: those who think wraps can do anything and those who think wraps will fall off the vehicle while driving down the road. Here we go into some of the most common misconceptions about wraps.

Paint Damage

Vehicle wraps are not harmful to your paint if they are installed properly with high-quality films. Much of the lore around vinyl wrap and paint damage is due to old versions of the film as well as installers themselves damaging vehicles.

In the past, films and adhesives were not as complex as they are today. They stuck so strongly to the surface that they did remove paint when they were being removed. 3M holds training classes where vehicles are wrapped and unwrapped hundreds of times without any paint damage. Installers also have a part to play. If your cut procedure is wrong, you will cut and damage the paint. There is no myth about that.

High Cost

Vinyl wraps are extremely inexpensive and so are the materials.

When considering color-change options, few are more cost effective than vinyl wrap. The other true alternative is paint, which is much more expensive. If you are a DIYer, there are many more tools and facilities that are required to paint.

Vinyl wrap usually runs $600 to $900 a roll, which is enough to wrap almost any car. Pair that with a few tools under $200, and you can have a wrapped car.

Some think that wraps are cheap. Installers are in high demand, and good ones require a premium wage. To have someone with skill wrap your vehicle is not cheap. We also recommend the complete disassembly of a vehicle for a professional wrap. Disassembling cars requires a person of skill. Wraps in the United States can range from $1,500 to $15,000.

Durability

Although it is not indestructible, vinyl wrap has some durability. It is the first line of defense for the vehicle's paint and does a wonderful job of protecting it.

Difficult Removal

A good-quality wrap will take time to install, but it is not difficult or complex to remove. In Arizona, we pull the vehicle into the sun on a hot day, let it bake for a few hours, and start peeling. No matter your location, you can go panel by panel with a heat gun the same way.

VINYL GRAPHICS USES AND APPLICATIONS

This may look like a paint job with a lot of decals, but it's actually a full-printed vehicle.

Vinyl graphics have been around for a long time. They can be applied on many surfaces, including windows, walls, trucks, buses, etc. Vinyl graphics are cool because any image can be printed. Simply design a proper image, scale it to size, and your creation comes alive.

Graphics are mostly used for business applications to advertise and professionalize company cars. Think about the landscaping truck you saw at the home improvement store today, or the full-color wrapped beverage delivery truck. Chances are good that if you go to the store right now, you can find at least a few examples of graphic-wrapped vehicles.

However, that is not the only use for vinyl graphics. We create custom graphics all the time. Camos, galaxy wraps, and race branding designs are a few of the more popular options.

This vehicle's white paint with decals and prints gives it the appearance of having a full wrap. This is a clever design for the client to save on materials and still get a full-billboard look.

Print versus Plot

Printing is exactly as it sounds: a print job. However, instead of printing onto a sheet of paper, the image is printed onto specialty print vinyl and laminated to protect the print. Laminate is a thin see-through film that is placed on top of the print. These prints can be as large as the film and printer allow.

Plotting is the cutting of the vinyl. This can be for printed films or premanufactured color films. Both processes require design and production skills to accomplish. Plotted vinyl can often be seen on the side of work vans as lettering or a logo. Think of plotting as a precise knife. It will cut any shape, but the only thing that a plotter can do is cut films to shape.

Full Wraps

Many graphic-style prints are used to wrap a full vehicle exactly to the size of the vehicle's panels. When a work truck or car is wrapped in a graphic, the result is a moving billboard. The install process and skills learned in this book are similar for both color-change and graphic prints.

A full wrap with graphics is like a full color-change wrap. A "full wrap" means that the exterior body painted components are fully wrapped in film. In the color-change vinyl world, some people like to have the inside of their doors, or doorjambs, wrapped in the same material as the outside.

This can even flow into the trunk and all the open interior body painted panels of the car. This is almost never done with graphics since the goal is most often to advertise a business, where only the exterior of the vehi-

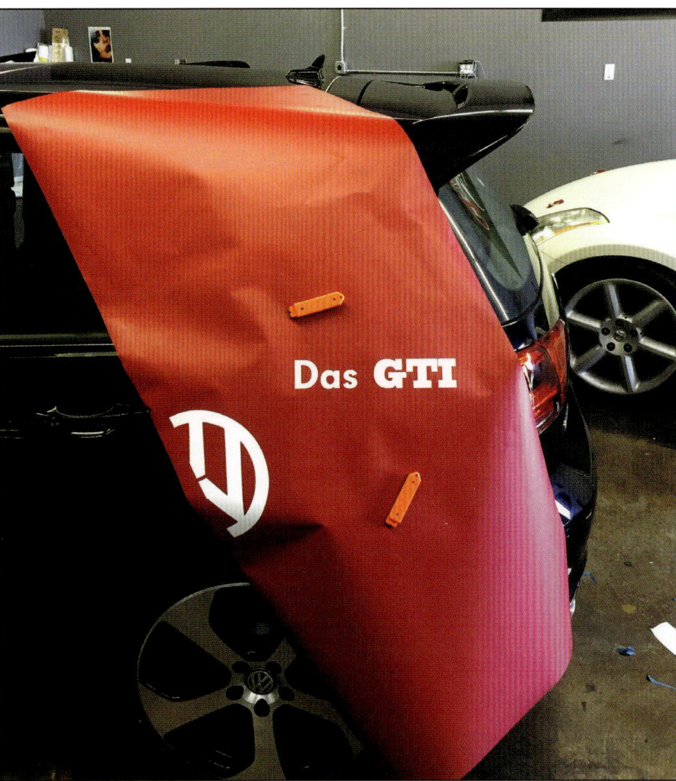

On this GTI, the basis of the plotted graphic is being mocked-up for placement. This is a graphic wrap but also a full panel like a color-change wrap. The VW logo must be perfectly placed on the vehicle's natural panel break to give the illusion of a runoff. Mocking up the graphic like this helps visualize the placement before installation.

With the vinyl now laid on the vehicle, the black paint is exposed through the plotted holes to create a graphic effect.

cle is addressed. When you think about a color-change wrap, they are primarily used to style your car; with graphics, the goal is to advertise.

Partial Wraps

Similar to full wraps, graphics are applied to the vehicle to either customize or advertise. Great design skills come in handy here because it is possible to make the paint of your vehicle flow with a graphic. If this is done well, it can give the illusion of a full wrap with a cost savings.

Partial wraps can be anything from half the car to the tailgate or a simple decal. Most often, clever designers can make a design flow so well the paint can actually add to the excitement of the wrap. It is also possible to just wrap a back window and get a lot of value.

Windows are generally wrapped in perforation (perf) film, which is visible like a solid sign from the outside but completely see-through from inside of the vehicle. Up close, perf films look like they have hundreds of tiny holes in them. Perf films can also be popular in full wraps and allow a true full-wrap look that includes all the windows.

This HP Latex 360 printer is capable of printing on many various substrates, but our favorite is high-quality wrap film. Machines such as this can make anything designed on computer screen come to life on a vehicle.

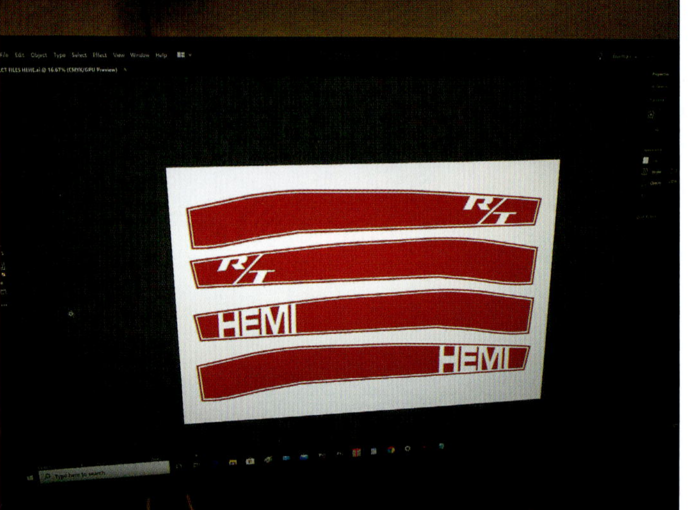

This is the production of vinyl graphics. It all starts with designs. We tell the highly technical equipment the job to perform. This is done in a design and layout phase. This is also a good chance to send a photo to the client and show him or her what you intend to produce. You can also splash the graphic on an actual picture to show the client what his or her vehicle will look like. Design skills are useful in the wrap industry.

Plotted Graphics

In commercial applications, plotted graphics are often only on the door of a vehicle. This may even involve a single-color logo to help further brand the vehicle. It is also possible to first print and then plot a graphic to give it a multiple-color option but still cut around the graphic.

On personal vehicles, there are racing-stripe kits, such as those found on a Ford Mustang. A popular setup is two 1-inch-wide racing stripes down the entire center of the vehicle or brand decals, such as Brembo or Flowmaster. These are examples of plotted graphics.

Vinyl Printing: Methods and Tools

There are many film options that are pre-produced and available from manufacturers of film, such as 3M or Avery Dennison. The exciting and great thing about vinyl is that you do not have to stick to pre-produced designs. With access to a large-format printer, anything that a person can imagine and design can be printed. This includes any color. In addition, with access to more and more laminates, this can include an increasing number of finishes. In short, the sky is the limit for printing and producing films.

However, access to large-format printers may not happen overnight because they are expensive. Also, high-powered computers, lamina-

A laminator is a key tool for printing vehicle wraps. After the design is printed, the ink must be sealed in and protected. The lamination layer is added after the film is printed and involves a separate machine, such as the one pictured. There are many various types of laminators that range in price from the low thousands to the high thousands of dollars.

One of the best tools that a wrap shop can have is a great large-format plotter. This Graphtec plotter will cut Clear Bra kits, decals, and much more. This can save hours and eliminate the need to use knifeless tape with a stripe kit. Think of this machine as a large, accurate cutting machine. In many of the examples shown in this book, this is the machine that performed the job.

tors, and many types of software are required. It will take time to become proficient with the design and production software. Some programs do both. Most often, the design is created with Adobe Illustrator and then transferred to Production, which is a program used to size and print the wrap.

Many companies, such as HP, Mutoh, and Roland, produce large-format printers and laminators. These printers can use solvent-based ink or latex ink. There are many pros and cons to the printers and ink types. Decisions to use one type or the other can be made by personal preference or cost. By the time that this book is completed, printers may have changed so drastically that any advice given here will be out of date. Technology moves quickly. So, talk to a few of the major players and do your research before you buy.

Latex Printer

We currently have a large-format latex printer that we like because it allows us to go straight to lamination from print with no real ink-dry time. With some printers, it is necessary to allow for what's called "outgassing," or allowing time for the ink to dry before the lamination step of printing. So, do not seal in a wet print that is still releasing moisture under the laminate.

Laminators are large devices with rollers that lay a clear protective layer over your vinyl print. This lamination is what protects the ink in the print over the long term. A good printer will cost at least $20,000, and a laminator costs about $5,000 to $10,000.

Vinyl Plotting: Methods and Tools

A vinyl plotter is a bit more attainable in the initial stages of working with film. This is because it is much less expensive and can be versatile. It is a great tool for cutting films.

Just like a printer, a vinyl plotter requires the use of a computer, software, and the creativity and knowledge to design and produce the plotted film. It can run from a few hundred dollars to thousands.

One can cut only as large as the machine, and the machines come in many various sizes. The width of the machine is roughly the width of the film that can be cut, but the length can be miles long. It is hypnotic to watch a plotter run its cutting profile. It's so quick and precise. A plotter can be used for racing-stripe kits, such as the ones on calipers, or even window stickers. Imagine that you were as good as a machine at cutting and you took a single-color piece of stock film and cut it with your knife. That is the same basic idea as a plotted decal.

Purchasing Preprinted and Plotted Vinyl

There are many different options to access printed and plotted vinyl. Many companies sell pre-manufactured racing-stripe kits or decals. There are even places where you can send your files to have them printed onto vinyl. As with color-change vinyl, be careful of the types of film that these types of dealers are selling.

For instance, some online vendors sell racing-stripe kits made from inferior-quality vinyl. Print and plot vinyl can be of low or high quality, just like any other film. Make sure to ask questions and get products that are for high-end vehicle application, such as Avery Supreme or the 3M 1080 series.

Printed vinyl films also have tiers of quality. There is cheap low-quality print vinyl and there is expensive print vinyl. The cost of the vinyl usually correlates to having a better air-channel system for installation, a better adhesive for removal, and improved film longevity.

Working with a Vinyl Print Shop

Working with a vinyl print shop is a good alternative to buying online. Many vinyl print shops will let a customer bring in film to be cut into stripes or decals. Others allow you to send them your files that they will print for you. Many will require that the files are formatted and designed for production, but they will certainly help you with these steps for an additional fee.

Another option is to hire an outside designer to create the artwork

A fully designed layout will help the print shop nail down an accurate quote.

to be printed at the print shop. However, be careful. Just because someone is a designer does not mean they will be able to design your artwork in the exact way the print shop wants it produced. The best vehicle-wrap designers also have experience installing the film, as they know how to allow for certain tendencies in problematic areas on vehicles. As you design, keep in mind that vehicles are not completely flat. They have inlays and outlays that must be accounted for in the design. It is also important to make sure that the graphic is formatted per the vehicle's specifications, and the designer should allow for a bit of bleed (extra material) at the ends.

Develop a good relationship with a print shop, and it will reap dividends in the end. We suggest selecting one with a reputation of high-quality work. Review the shop's online portfolio to see the type of clients and designs that they have completed in the past. Choosing a print shop that specializes in high-quality wraps is the best option.

BEFORE YOU GET STARTED

With vinyl, many variables can make the job easier or harder. We have been through them all. The techniques, tips, and informative tool insight in this chapter will set you up for success.

If you have worked on a car before, you know how the materials, preparation, and environment dictate the outcome of any job. Before beginning a project, it is important to know how to make your job easier. Simple tips, such as having an extra set of hands around, will make all the difference in the ease of your install and quality of the outcome.

Materials

As with many other products in the automotive world, there are different options when it comes to film. There are also a variety of film manufacturers. Well-known brands make both premium and entry-level products. Premium films are usually directly created for high-end vehicle application, much like the processes in this book.

However, beware. Just because it's called "vinyl wrap" does not mean that it's made for a vehicle application. We also caution about manufacturers who present their products as premium products but fall short when it comes to actual installation and quality. We will discuss cheap materials and why you shouldn't use them.

In the car world, there Geo Metros and Lamborghinis, and it is easy to tell the two apart. Don't expect a Geo Metro to go 0 to 60 in less than 4 seconds. However, with film, it may look the same at first glance, but it can cause a whirlwind of problems down the road.

The two most important components to a film are also what sets the manufacturers apart. First is the exterior layer, which gives it the look, durability, and, to some extent, longevity. Second is the interior adhesive layer, which allows the film to adhere to the vehicle. Look for an adhesive

Avery Dennison Supreme Film Satin Orange is used on the hood of this vehicle. There is plenty of film left over to trim back.

These 3M 1080 plotted decals for these racers were built on our Graphtec 8600 plotter. They are a quite simple design. A single-color film and plotter are the only items required for a project such as this.

that is amazingly strong but also will heat release when the time comes to unwrap or reposition a panel.

It is also important that the residue of the adhesive does not immediately dislodge onto the vehicle and cause a mess and an impossible reposition. In the vehicle wrap world, it is imperative to get a film that can be repositioned. It makes your job a hundred times harder if you have to lay every panel in one shot.

Outer Layer

The outer layer is what's on stage. This is the visible layer. Not only is it important that the film looks good but it also needs to be as durable as paint and last more than a week. Some poor-quality films will have hazing, which looks like a mist or fog over the finish. They may have banding, which is a result of poor manufacturing and means that the color didn't flow all the way evenly. The color will appear as lighter and darker bands of the same color. Should you see any of these items, don't use the film and return it.

As with any manufacturing, flaws can be in the film itself. We even heard of a fly being stuck to the

This 3M 1080 full-vehicle wrap in satin dark grey has gloss black accents. A lot of our clients love a bit of contrast. Using a satin film in combo with a gloss can really make the accents pop. Vehicle manufacturers spend millions of dollars designing vehicles. If you can follow the overall vision yet tweak with textures and colors, the results can be awesome and flow well.

adhesive layer and wrapped up in the roll. However, most often there are fold marks or roll bunching.

The look of the film is what we are here for. If you have good film, there should be no way to tell between it and a high-quality painted panel. A good outer layer will not easily show stretch lines or banding lines. Good materials will be easier to work with, 100 percent removable after application, and not damage your OEM paint.

Inferior films will quickly break down in poor conditions. They are more susceptible to sun and element damage. On average, a film should last years, not months. Choose the wrong film, and a few months down the road the film may crack and require days of cleanup and maybe cause body/paint damage. Think of cracking as the sand on the beach: it will first dehydrate and then crack without water. If you remove the film, you will be picking it off thousands of tiny little pieces.

Recommendations

We advise sticking to two major brands: 3M and Avery Dennison. These are the two films we have used the most over the years. Both offer a multitude of options and have films

   HOW TO VINYL WRAP CARS, TRUCKS, & MOTORCYCLES

that are easy with which to work, are beautiful in appearance, and possess quality adhesives. Both brands compete for having the best-quality product on the market, and they care about their films' abilities to last in any condition as well as reverse easily and remove. This is especially important when it comes to removal years down the road.

If this is your first time applying vinyl, you might think that all carbon-fiber black films are the same and that the one that costs the least amount of money is your best bet. However, during the learning curve, it is more imperative than ever to have an easily workable film. Make sure to use reputable films and dealers. Films have shelf lives and can be much harder to work with when they are expired. Use only reliable websites and sign shops, such as Fellers.

Preparation

After film choice, preparation is perhaps the most important component to your success and being the envy of your car club. The test of the great install is telling someone that

At 3M, the door handles are removed from the car to get a perfect result. Door handles are difficult to wrap. They take a lot of time and patience, and having them not attached to the car makes it a much easier task.

it's a wrap and watching them try to find a sign. A great installer will not leave any clues as to how the car was wrapped and not painted.

It's all in the prep. How many times has everyone heard this? Be it paint, a roofing job, or setting up for an interview. Preparation is a key factor in most tasks and it's no different here. But in this instance, a speck of dust, a piece of hair, and every fingerprint can be detrimental to a perfect install.

Be prepared to spend a lot of time during this step. We have a saying in vinyl: "If you can feel it, you can see it." A contaminant will turn into an

This is a close-up of a 3M 1080 Satin Smoldering Red Audi hood. How did we wrap the hood with that badge on there? We took it off. Years ago, when wraps were first coming out, people wrapped around and over everything, including badges. That is not the way to do a good job. After all, would you paint a vehicle with the badge on? The absolute best way to get a great result is by removing this badge and replacing it with a brand new one. There is nothing better than the adhesive on the back of a new badge. The old one can be used but the old adhesive needs to be removed and replaced with aftermarket adhesive tape, and it's never quite good as the real thing.

ugly, visible defection. The preparation stage is also the time to consider what you will do with any paint and

Here is a 3M 1080 Gloss Black mirror wrap. Mirrors are one of the harder items on the vehicle to wrap. All mirrors require a different approach. A lot of first-time installers will do pretty well with a vehicle wrap until it gets to the mirrors and bumpers. It's important to use the stretch ability of the film but not overstretch.

A 3M 1080 Satin Dark Grey full wrap is shown with gloss black accents. There are also color-match wheels and a badge to go with it. This car uses several products in harmony for an awesome result.

We will always advocate powder coating as the best choice for wheels over the long term. Paint is truly the best tool for the job when it comes to badges. It is much easier to color match this way as well. A good painter can match just about any color.

---

bodywork discrepancies. If you have rock chips, the film will not bond. Prepare the surface by filling in the chips to make them no longer visible.

Deep scratches will stand out as if the film was not there at all. This is not a book about bodywork, but there are several ways to address bodywork and paint decisions prior to vinyl install. Some items can be wet sanded, while others must be filled, primered, and resprayed prior to vinyl application.

If you have a brand-new vehicle, it may not require bodywork but still need prep work. Prep work is required every time and all the time. This is a large variable in your equation to install a perfect wrap.

Environment

Where will the project take place? Will the vinyl wrap be installed outdoors? Will it be installed in a garage or a maintenance bay at work? What's the lighting like? How well is the area cleaned and maintained? What are the temperatures in the installation area?

Think of wrap as similar to paint when answering these questions. The best paint jobs are made in controlled environments. Paint booths have temperature control, ventilation systems, and plenty of light. We sometimes use a booth in our installs. This is perfect-scenario stuff. If you don't have paint booth access, the following are good alternatives and what should be done to prep the environment.

Dirt and dust contaminants are some of the biggest factors in a bad wrap job. Just as a doctor requires a sterile environment, your operation will as well. Wraps are prone to static electricity. The moment the backing is removed, the vinyl will suck up hair and contaminants like a tractor beam. You must clean your environment: sweep, mop, and prep the floors, and wipe down walls near the installation area. Don't let dogs or people in the area after it has been cleaned. Installers wear long shirts to avoid arm hairs from falling onto the application area during installation.

Temperature control is also important. If your environment is too hot, the film will become soft and hard to work with. Almost like a gelatinous glue, it will lose shape and stretch too easily. Overheating and stretching can cause white stretch marks in the film. If it's too cold, the film can become brittle and break while you are stretching it. The perfect temperature will allow you to work with the film the way it is intended. The film should only be heated in situations that require it. The ambient heat temperature in the room should be 75° to 80°F, and the film should be heated to 135°F during installation.

Lights are important for spotting contaminants, wrinkles, and other detrimental issues. Many people do not own the latest 40,000-lumen shop lights, but there are several things you can do. Hardware and home improvement stores sell light-emitting diode (LED) light

Avery Supreme Gloss Yellow is shown with 3M 1080 Gloss Black accents. This is an example of using two high-gloss films in unison to make something eye turning. The wonderful thing about film is if you choose two you can literally make the car look 100 different ways. As you can see here, the mirrors and the hood are matched instead of making them body colored.

This is a 3M 1080 Gloss Raspberry Fizz full-vehicle wrap. We are almost always asked to do something beyond a simple full wrap. This is a true example of just a full wrap. Only the body's painted components are wrapped. We think of a wrap a lot like a paint job. Certainly, the chrome and wheels would not be included in a standard paint job. We offer a full wrap the same way.

A 3M IJ180 printed carbon-fiber wrap is shown on this spoiler. You can print anything imaginable, even a realistic-appearing carbon fiber.

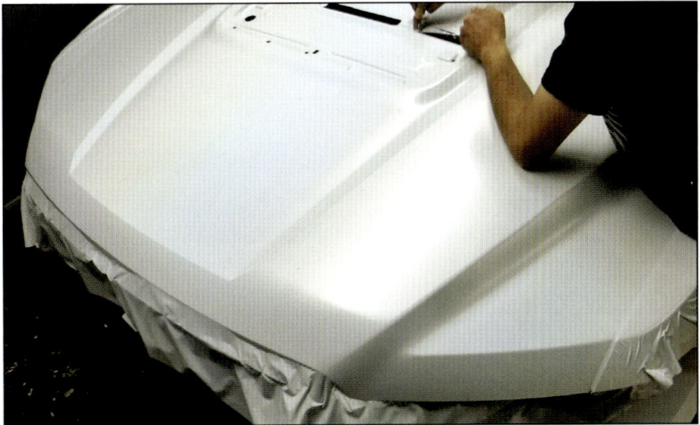

The hood-cutting procedure on this Raptor hood is in 3M Gloss Flip Ghost Pearl. The hood is disman-tled so that the film can be tucked all the way under the accent items. When film is just laid, it will not fit the item perfectly. The leftover film will appear as fringe-like in the front of the picture. It is up to a wrapper to know how to trim all this back to perfection.

stands for over-the-shoulder light output. In a poor light environment, many installers also use headlamps to see what they are doing. Replacing the bulbs with LED clean white light bulbs can improve the lighting in your install area.

Don't get us wrong—you can install film in the backyard of a swap meet using a credit card for a squeegee, but it will be hard to get a good result. A well-cleaned, mopped garage with climate control is an easily available install site for the DIYer.

Asking for Help

It is possible to wrap a vehicle alone, but having a partner when you start installing the wrap will make your job much easier. If you cannot get a person to help you for the entirety of the install, having someone around for key times is invaluable. If you have two people to assist, it will be even better. The best results can be attained with three people.

There are ways to go about this alone, such as attaching the vinyl and peeling away the backing while you stretch it down the rest of the vehicle, but it is much easier to have someone hold each side of the vinyl and another person pull the backing. As mentioned in the single-installer example, a back roll with two people is almost as good. We advise having someone available for at least the initial lay of large panels. If you are alone, you can do it by pulling back the end of the film, slightly tacking it to the panel, and pulling off the backing while you walk the rest of the panel. However, this is much harder to do.

Cutting

Yes, knives are used to cut the vinyl on cars valued at $100,000, but the vinyl is not cut while it is on the car. Cutting is one of the more artistic components to the vehicle-wrap trade. After years in business, we have seen it all.

One example that we experienced was when another shop did a job for a client. The client was not happy with the bumper wrap, so the car was brought it to us to fix. When we removed the film, deep cut marks right through the clear coat were

An Avery Supreme Gloss Bahama Blue full wrap is shown with carbon-fiber accents. Gloss films have an appearance that is almost identical to paint. They can scratch like a gloss paint as well.

evident, which destroyed the expensive paint job underneath. Do not cut on the car.

Surfaces to Avoid

What's the paint like? Is it new, bad, a repaint, or for a car that was fresh off the dealer's lot? Wrap can be applied to the paint of OEM manufacturers hundreds of times and removed with no issues. In training classes, vehicles are wrapped over and over again only to have it removed and reveal the perfectly preserved paint underneath.

We have wrapped rental cars for events and removed the wrap the next day before the car was returned.

After OEM paint, the second-best surface option is an extremely high-quality repaint. Prep, paint quality, and cure time will all impact the possibility of paint pulling up. Yes, you can pull up paint! Wrap adhesives are so strong that they can rip a weak paint job off the vehicle. In rare cases, we have seen this happen with factory paint.

A bad repaint will leave clear coat on the back of the film, which will ruin the film and make a bodywork fix the only way to get a good result. This is also true of brand-new paint. We recommend waiting at least six weeks after a new paint job to attempt a wrap. If your paint is in bad condition, such as the clear coat is peeling back from age, you must perform bodywork to the vehicle before it is wrapped.

This wrap will get a decal-style design afterward. We hung the design photos on the window to have a game plan for the entire project.

Vinyl racks such as these are ideal for storing vinyl. Do not place it on the floor, which would create wear marks or pressure areas. Films should be installed in less than a year from their date. When a film is ordered, do so from a reputable supplier that will not sell films that have been stored for years. Temperature is important to film. It is important to store films in temperatures that are not too hot or cold.

Storage

Vinyl has a life span, and it's shorter on the roll than on the vehicle. Premium films are rated at two to seven years, but for roll storage, the recommendation is about a year.

It is important to find out when the roll was produced because if the film is stored above or below required temps, it can be detrimental to the film. An old film will have a poor adhesive quality and cause a mess for your wrap project.

APPLICATION PLANNING

As a vinyl wrap installer, the odds are good that you will experience situations that may seem to come out of nowhere and need a quick solution. This book is intended to help you get through these problems as they arise. Part of becoming a highly skilled installer is having the ability to decrease, and in most cases eliminate, these instances and get to the point where each install is virtually problem-free.

Being fully prepared before beginning any vinyl project will greatly increase the odds of a problem-free install. In this chapter, the main tools for your project and key things to remember when ordering material are provided. In addition, we cover how to analyze a panel and incorporate different installation techniques to solve issues before they arise when laying a panel.

Tools

There is a plethora of tools used when it comes to doing a full color change for example. We won't necessarily be going over the tools required to accomplish tasks, such as those in this chapter, but rather we'll focus more on the tools used regarding the installation of vinyl wrap film.

Squeegee

The trusty squeegee is the main workhorse out of all the tools used during any vinyl wrap install. It is a rectangular piece of hard plastic with a piece of felt attached on one end.

There are options available that come in various sizes and thicknesses. Squeegees can range in price from $6 to $16, and that range really reflects the quality difference of the felt and the durability of the plastic.

I wrap five days a week and can usually make one squeegee last about a month. For a tool that you will use regularly, it's worth getting the nice one. The squeegee that we prefer is the orange felt squeegee made by Geek Wraps. It is listed as the

Here are a few types of squeegees that are available. The blue and yellow squeegee in the upper right-hand corner is a little softer and will bend a little or flex as the installer applies pressure. The green squeegee at the top of the photo offers a rounded edge to allow the installer to get in close to curved areas. The pink squeegee at the bottom of the photo is much thinner than the others and can apply pressure into tight spaces.

This is the most-used squeegee at our shop. At an average price of $16, these squeegees are a bit pricey, but it's worth it having a nice tool to use every day. The white edge of this squeegee is firm and does not allow any give when lifting and tucking the vinyl into tight areas, such as under window trim and grille inserts. Keep the felt area clean and away from dusty surfaces, and this tool can last about 3 weeks to a month before it needs to be replaced.

Keep the Squeegee Clean

Never set the squeegee on the ground, the vehicle, or any other surface where it can pick up dust and other contaminants. The felt will attract dirt and eventually get to the point where it begins to scratch the surface of the vinyl during installation. ■

Like a squeegee, the heat gun will be used every day, so find one that has all the features that are needed.

Chrome Squeegee. Although is it one of the more expensive options out there, we like the softness and quality of felt that is used and find that it can be used for a long period of time before it needs to be replaced.

I always keep my squeegee in my back-left pocket when it's not being used so that I know where it is at all times. Squeegees are available in a myriad of various sizes. Some may be smaller and thinner to get into hard-to-reach places. Others may be wider and longer in length to cover more surface area.

Honestly, when I first began to wrap, I had a collection of squeegees of all the various sizes, but as my skills increased, I discovered that 90 percent of my wraps were completed just fine with one size. There is one other squeegee that comes to a point on one end that comes in handy when working with tight corners. Aside from that, I stick to the rectangular Geek Wraps squeegee.

Heat Gun

Another tool that is frequently used is a heat gun. Over the years I've discovered what constitutes a good heat gun when it comes to vinyl wrap installation.

First, it is important that you're able to operate the heat gun by only using one hand. You'll quickly discover that when you are installing vinyl-wrap film, eventually you will wish there were an extra set of hands to help with the project. Unfortunately, oftentimes someone else isn't around.

When it comes to purchasing a heat gun, find one that has a comfortable grip and can be turned on by using a flip switch, rather than one with a switch to move upward with a firm grip on the handle.

You want to be able to grab the gun with one hand and flip the switch to turn it on while holding a piece of vinyl with the other hand.

Choose a heat gun that comes with a high/low setting in regard to the volume of heated air coming out of the gun. In some cases, you want the gun to blow softer when heating up smaller areas of the vinyl and harder when heating larger areas.

In addition, I prefer a gun that comes with a dial that allows you to control the temperature of the heat being produced. There are many times when you need to be gentler with the film and want to turn down the heat a little. You will use the heat gun numerous times every day and time you wrap every panel, so it is going to be used frequently. Find a gun that has many of the options described but isn't too expensive. Chances are good that because you will be using it so much, it will need to be replaced every six months or so. If you're only wrapping a single vehicle, a gun with all of these variables is still recommended.

There are some corners and tight spaces that cannot be reached with a regular squeegee. It's a good idea to have a triangular squeegee. It won't be used regularly, but it is nice to have when you need it.

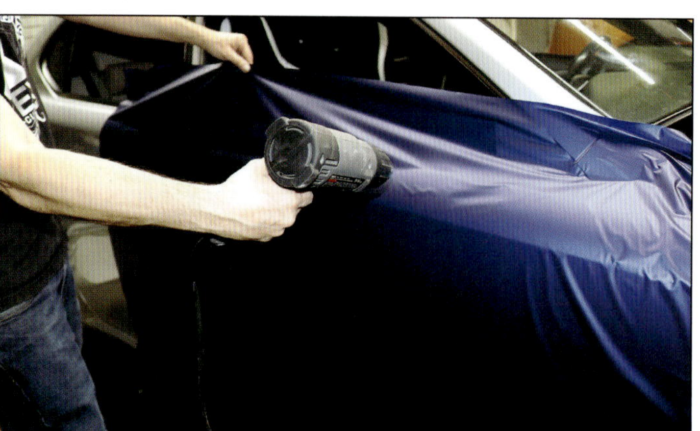

Choose a heat gun that can be operated with just one hand. There are many times when you need to use your other hand to simultaneously manipulate the vinyl.

Purchase a heat gun that offers variable speeds. A gun that offers a high/low option is really all that's needed. Some heat guns that have numerous speeds typically require you to use two hands, which is something that you want to avoid.

Find a heat gun with a built-in temperature dial. In many situations, you will want to increase or decrease the amount of heat. When heating a large panel, increase the heat. When removing tension lines on a piece of vinyl, cool it down a little.

This is the Olfa blade holder. It is the preferred tool by most vinyl installers. It is durable, easy to use, and long lasting. It is common to get a few years of use from it before it needs to be replaced.

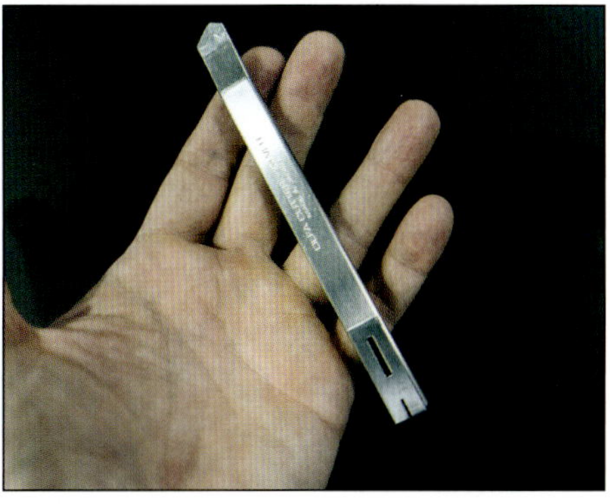

This is the back side of the Olfa knife holder. Although these can be purchased from your vinyl supplier, you can save money if you find them online. Websites typically offer them for around $8.

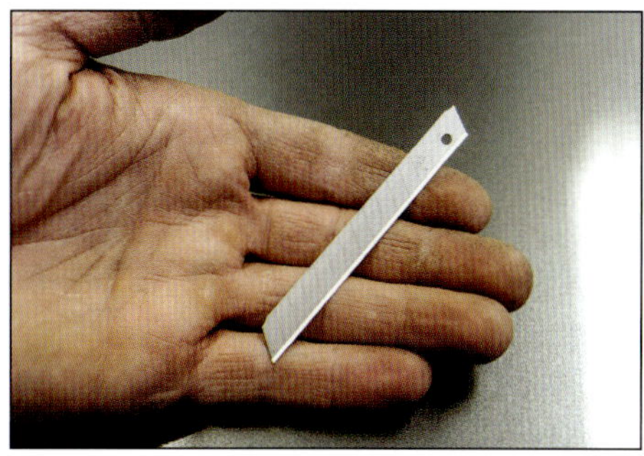

This is the stainless-steel Olfa replacement blade to use with the holder. We recommend it.

The Olfa blades break off in sections to provide a fresh sharp edge when needed. It is a good practice to do this as frequently as possible.

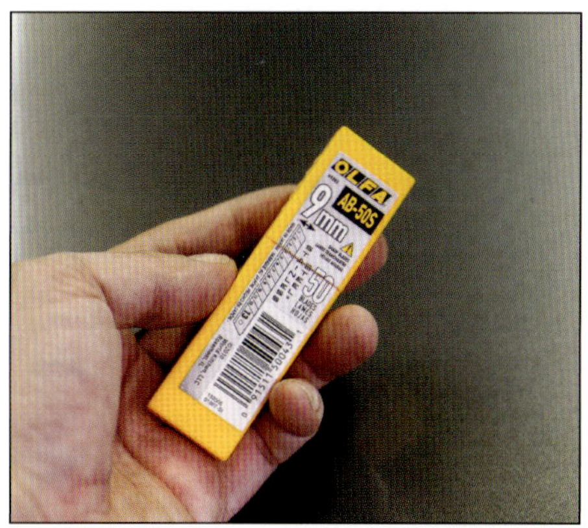

A pack of 50 replacement blades will average around $28. Order replacements when you're down to half of a pack.

A quality heat gun costs about $30 to $40. Always keep a new one handy as a backup because they are known to stop working without much warning as they get older. If you have a new backup on deck, you'll be able to continue with the project without delay.

Stainless Breakaway Steel Knife

Another tool that no vinyl wrap installer can do without is a knife. It will be used to cut large panel pieces off of the roll, pull up the edges of decals, trim down panels that were just installed, and numerous other situations. This tool is used so often that you will never want it to lose it.

As mentioned earlier, I made a habit of always keeping my squeegee in my left back pocket. I also always keep my blade in my right back pocket. Many new vinyl installers, myself included, have wasted precious time trying to find a blade. It is much easier to designate a place on your body where the blade goes each time it is not in use. Time is money!

We prefer the Olfa brand blade holder that uses the typical 9-mm replacement breakaway blades. The knife itself comes with a blade preloaded in it and will cost around $8.

The blades are designed to break off in sections to provide a sharp edge every time it is used. It is important that you do not attempt to cut with a dull knife because you will be tempted to apply a greater amount of pressure, which will increase the risk of cutting through the vinyl and possibly damaging the paint on a vehicle.

Because of this, frequently replace the blades and have plenty around. A pack of 50 replacement blades is typically about $28, and it is good to always have extra packs on hand. When it comes to choosing what blades to use, a few options are available. We highly recommend sticking with the 9-mm stainless-steel blade that has a 59-degree angle. There's also a black carbon blade that is sharper but will also etch glass, so it is not recommended for beginners.

Those who are just starting out should steer clear of the 30-degree blade. These are good for cutting around corners in the hands of an experienced wrapper, but since they have a finer point at the tip, some beginners may find that they are too sharp and might be more harmful than good.

Knifeless Tape

Knifeless tape is truly an ingenious invention. It's a lot of fun to use, comes in handy, and can often become one of the favorite tools to use in a wrapper's arsenal. It comes in a small, handheld roll and consists of a narrow green strip that contains a thin cord running down the middle of it.

There comes a time when an installer needs to cut a specific line or pattern in the vinyl but the line is too precise to be cut by freehanding it with a blade. It is handy in situations

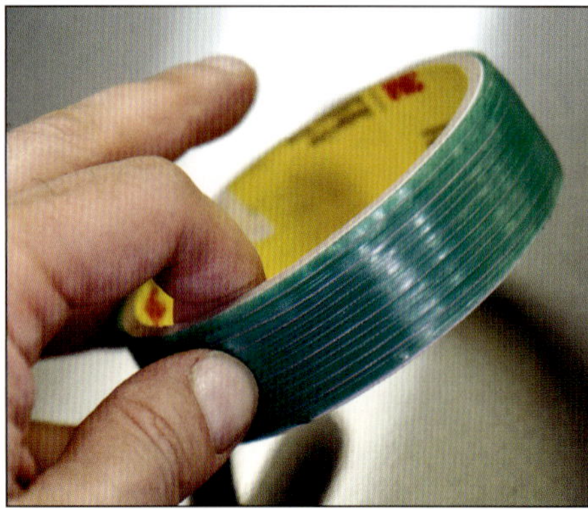

Always keep at least one roll of 3M Design Line knifeless tape in the toolbox.

where the installer wants a piece of vinyl to follow a certain body line on the vehicle or when incorporating a seam that must appear as straight as possible. The cord that runs through the middle of the tape will be pulled and used to cut through the vinyl, so the exact line that the tape runs will be the cut line as well.

The tape goes down first, and the installer can pull it up and correct its path until it meets the formation of the line. The vinyl is then installed over the knifeless tape. Once that piece is fully installed, the wrapper can pull the cord and watch it cut through the exact predetermined path that the installer created.

Infrared Heat Lamp

Having access to an infrared heat lamp can be extremely helpful when it comes to laying vinyl wrap film, especially when it comes to certain types of panels. A heat lamp is an excellent way to apply hands-free heat to a piece of vinyl prior to and during install.

There are a few situations when it comes in handy, and one is while wrapping bumpers. The most efficient way to install a bumper is to use a two-person approach with an installer on each end of the piece of vinyl. With the lamp on and positioned to face the middle of the bumper, both installers can lay both ends without having to pick up a heat gun. The entire bumper can be installed solely by using the heat from the lamp, which allows each installer to focus on the stretching and placement of the material as the installers work their way to complete each end.

We find the heat lamp to be most useful on panels containing curves. Curved panels, such as trunks and fenders, can be tricky for an installer and often require a nice horizontal stretch on them, so they hug the panel without any built-up excess in the vinyl.

The knifeless tape is placed on the vehicle before the panel is installed. Once the material has been installed, pull the string through the vinyl to execute a clean, straight cut without using a blade.

An infrared heat lamp is commonly used to heat a piece of vinyl before it is applied to the vehicle.

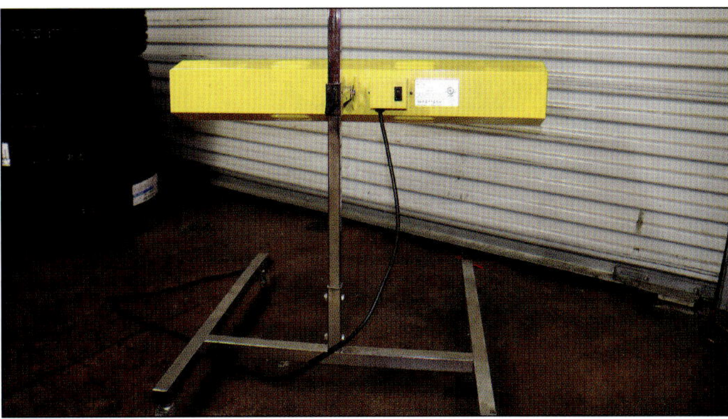

This is a rear view of the infrared heat lamp. By pulling outward on the black knob in the back, the lamp can be raised and lowered to meet the height of the panel being installed.

To do this, we recommend using a two-person approach whenever possible. Once the panel is clean and ready to be laid, each installer will position themselves at either end of the panel. With the lamp facing the panel, the installers peel off the backing while they stand between the lamp and the panel.

With the backing removed, the installers hold the piece of vinyl about a foot in front of the lamp and move the piece to apply an even amount of heat throughout the entire piece of vinyl.

Once the vinyl is heated, the two installers approach the panel until it is hovering a few inches away from the vehicle. At this point, the installers initiate a slight stretch on the piece as they lay the vinyl onto the car. Stretching the vinyl prior to making contact is what I refer to as using a horizontal stretch, which allows the piece to hug the panel and result in a wrinkle-free piece that is ready to be squeegeed with a limited number of adjustments.

Heat is used to soften the vinyl prior to its application. Heat allows the vinyl to better conform to the shape of the vehicle.

Two installers are placing a horizontal stretch on a piece of vinyl as it is being installed.

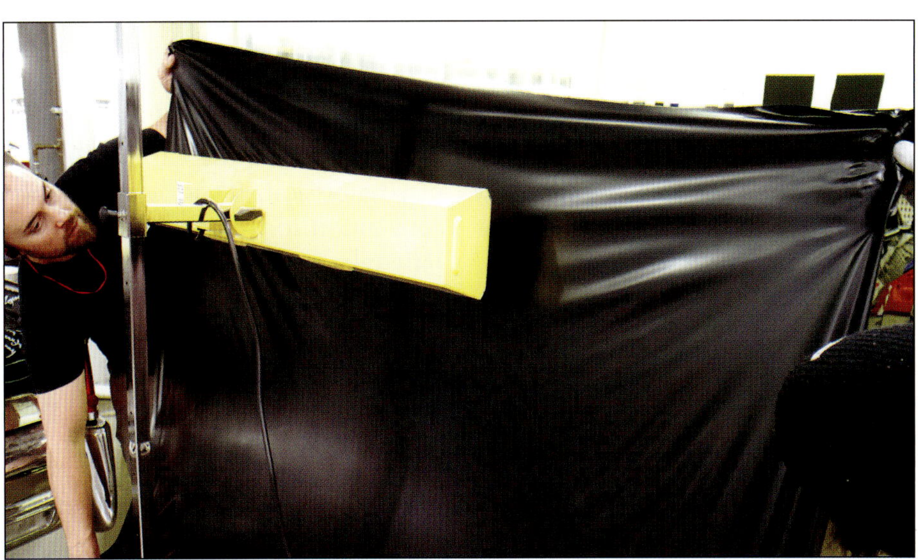

The vinyl seems to really love the gentle heat that an infrared lamp produces and gives it that soft pliable feel that is perfect for installation. As far as necessities go in regard to tools, lamps are more of a luxury item but can prove to be extremely useful.

Use caution when using the heat lamp. Proper distancing is important. Keep the lamp approximately 2 to 3 feet away from the panel you are wrapping. Duration is also key. There is no need to have a lamp on in front of a panel for any more than 5 or 10 minutes. Have the panel clean and ready to be installed prior to turning on your lamp. A plastic panel can be much more susceptible to heat, so never leave a heat lamp on and unattended in front of these panels.

The tools mentioned above are fairly inexpensive, and with a clean working environment, you can theoretically wrap a full car with just the items in this section. Now, let's focus on the actual material needed to complete a wrap project.

Quantity, Cost, and Time Estimates

For those just starting out, it can be difficult to determine how much material is needed to complete a project. This section will not only help you figure that out but will also go over the cost and approximate time needed to complete your project. So, let's begin with the amount of material needed.

Material

Most major brands follow the same guidelines when it comes to the size in which their vinyl wrap is sold. The vinyl will be wrapped around a cardboard core and will typically be 60 inches or 5 feet in width from left to right. If you purchase a full roll, the length will be 25 yards (75 feet) in length. If you are performing a full color change and your goal is to wrap the entire vehicle, most cars can be completed with one full roll. This will give the installer enough material to wrap the vehicle and may allow for one or two panels to be rewrapped in case there is mishap with a panel or two during installation.

The cost for one full roll of most films in a gloss, matte, or satin finish will typically be around $600. If your project requires a specialty color, such as one that shifts, or has a unique finish, such as a carbon-fiber film or brushed finish, the cost can be anywhere from $700 to $1,000, respectively. Be aware beforehand of these upcharges for specialty vinyl, and plan accordingly when budgeting the cost of materials.

Chrome films are the most expensive to purchase, as they typically cost three times the amount of films with a normal finish. On average, the amount of chrome film that is necessary to wrap an entire vehicle will cost $2,000. The average time it takes two novice installers to complete a full color change is approximately four or five days. However, two experienced wrappers will be able to cut that install time down to about two to three days. You should know how long the car will be out of commission. It's a common misconception to think a full wrap will only take a day or two when you are a novice.

Partial Wraps

There will be times when your project will not call for a full wrap and you may have clients who request for only a specific panel to be wrapped. In this case, many clients often look to wrap these panels in some kind of black color. They may want to wrap a hood or a roof. If your goal is to do a large volume of these types of wraps, it's a good practice to have a roll of gloss, satin, and matte black film on hand (if you have the means) so that you will always have the material needed to complete these projects.

The demand for matte black film diminishes over the years, so even if you are able to keep gloss and satin black in stock, you will be able to fill most of clients' requests. If you are not able to keep this amount on hand, order material for each individual project. Be aware that there is a certain amount of risk in doing so because it will not allow for any mistakes to be made.

When ordering material for a single hood or roof and the vehicle is not on hand to measure prior to ordering, know that 9 feet (3 yards) will be a sufficient amount to cover most hoods and roofs. The approximate cost for each of these panels will put you around $90. You can cut costs if you have specific measurements when ordering the film.

Chrome Trim Wrap

When wrapping only the chrome trim of a vehicle, it can usually be accomplished with approximately 6 feet (2 yards) of film. The cost of material for a project this size will be around $60. The time it will take two novice wrappers is about a day and a half. Two experienced installers can complete a project like this in one day.

Stripes

If the client requests to have a stripe kit installed, it will depend on the nature of the stripes to be installed. A typical stripe kit that

A vinyl-wrap stripe kit, such as the one shown here, is a great way to dramatically improve the look of a vehicle. The key to making it look professional will greatly depend on taking accurate measurements and lining up the stripes correctly. If the stripes are off, even by a quarter inch, the inaccuracy will be noticeable. Start with the hood and find the exact center mark at the top and the bottom of the panel. Use a roll of masking tape that mimics the width of the gap in between the stripes and run the tape down the center of the hood. Double-check the measurements with your tape line. This line will be your guide during the install. Before beginning, stand back from the hood 6 or 7 feet and make sure the tape line is straight. If you need, make small adjustments until it is a nice straight line. Use that tape line as you install each stripe on either side of the tape.

Obstacles may interfere with the stripe kit install. Remove parts, such as washer pumps on the hood, and the antenna shown here. Attempting to wrap around parts that are located within the stripe's path can result in unwanted tension marks in the vinyl.

Accurate measurements will ensure that the stripes are placed perfectly in the center of each panel. Here, the antenna was removed prior to the install. Notice how each stripe hits the antenna in same location on either side. An appropriately centered stripe kit is a surefire way to achieve the amazing look of a professionally installed project.

consists of two 12-inch stripes down both front and rear bumpers will require approximately 12 feet (4 yards) of material. The cost of material will be around $130 and take two novice installers approximately 1½ days. Two experienced installers will be able to complete a project like this in less than one day.

These are a few of the common projects that clients may ask you to perform, and it will give you a good idea of the amount of material, cost, and time needed to complete the project.

Measuring and Mapping the Surface

There are times when you already have the required material to complete a project or have the luxury of measuring the vehicle prior to ordering the material. In these cases, here are a few pointers on how to take proper measurements from certain panels of the vehicle.

It is common to see a novice vinyl wrapper who is overly concerned with saving material to cut down on cost at the risk of making a panel unnecessarily difficult to install. When measuring a panel, an inexperienced installer may only give themselves an extra inch or two larger than the actual size of the panel. When it comes time to install the piece that has been cut so close to the size of the panel, it is easy to

An installer measures the width of a hood prior to cutting the material from the roll to have an accurate amount of material to cut.

Always remember to add 6 inches to both ends of the panel to reduce issues and increase the ease of installation.

come up short on one side. This can lead to the panel being scrapped and result in losing the entire piece of material.

On a flat panel, such as a roof or a hood, give yourself 5 to 6 inches of extra film in all four directions to allow for a much easier initial lay and reduce the chance of wasting the whole piece during install.

Pay attention to curved panels, such as bumpers and fenders. For example, a fender that is curved will need to be stretched a little toward the top of the panel. Areas like these require extra film to reduce finger-ing and give the film enough room to withstand the stretch. Because of this, give yourself 8 extra inches when measuring curved sections.

Remember, when you are taking measurements, go larger in most cases. Trying to save a few inches may force you to rewrap the entire panel.

Purchasing Material

Most of our vinyl material is purchased from a company named Fellers, which is the world's largest wholesale vinyl supply company. It was founded in 1986 and is based in Tulsa, Oklahoma. Its website is fellers.com. Here, you can sign up for a free account by filling in the required information and creating a username and password.

Once you create an account, order a few sample books of vinyl. These come in handy and provide examples to show to your clients when it comes to choosing certain colors and finishes for projects. Look through the sample books and become familiar with the various types of vinyl being offered so that you can recommend them to your clients.

Be aware that many of the colors will look different when they are exposed to sunlight, so if your client comes across a specific film in which they are interested, take the sample outside to see what it will look like under the sun. Often, the client has already decided that he or she wants to wrap the car, but selecting a color may be difficult because there are so many choices.

In cases like these, help the client narrow down his or her choices by finding out what finish is preferred. In many cases, it is easy to find out if the

When cutting a piece of vinyl to wrap a bumper that curves inward at the top, add an additional 8 inches from the panel break. This will give the installer the extra material needed to pull and stretch around the curve without fingering.

client prefers a gloss, satin, or matte finish. In doing so, two-thirds of the colors offered will be eliminated, which will greatly help the client make a final decision. Once the client knows exactly which color he or she wants, confidently place your order, knowing the client has selected the exact color needed for their project.

Whether it is Fellers or another supplier from which you choose to order your vinyl, know that most will require you to order by the yard. Each yard is equal to three feet, so do the math beforehand. Have the sample book on hand so that you can confirm the name of the material that you are ordering.

If you intend to wrap a full vehicle, one full roll (25 yards) is required. If you live in a populated area, chances are good that a large supplier, such as Fellers, may have the film available locally. If not, find out how the film will be delivered to you and how long it will take to arrive. Have the film on hand before the client arrives with the vehicle so that the project can start immediately.

Anticipating High-Tension Areas

Now that you have purchased the correct amount of material and the vehicle has arrived at your location, plan out which approaches you will take to carry out your wrap.

During this section, we will assume you are performing a full color change and will wrap the entire vehicle. Take a moment to walk around the vehicle and visualize the wrap going down on every panel. Although the film is advanced and is designed to flex into shallow recesses,

It is important to realize where the vinyl may encounter a high amount of tension during the install. This will help determine the best approach before you begin. Knowing where these areas are can help the installer decide whether an inlay is needed.

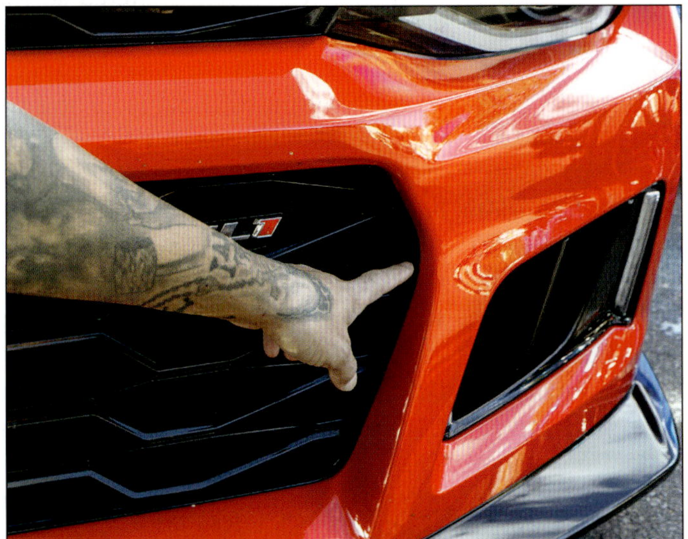

The area next to the grille is an area where the vinyl is under high tension.

The area shown here is also under a lot of tension. Although it may not require an inlay, the installer should take note of this section and lessen the tension by lifting the vinyl off the vehicle in this corner during the install. Refrain from forcing the material into corners like these.

There are several rear bumpers, such as these, that have a recessed area where the license plate is located. It is a good idea to examine these areas prior to install to come up with the best approach.

This is the recessed area next to the license plate. The installer is pointing to the area that will produce the greatest amount of tension to the vinyl. This will likely cause the material to lift if it is laid in one piece. to avoid this, place an inlay, a separate piece of vinyl, in this area prior to installing the main rear bumper piece. This will keep this section from failing, and it will add longevity to the wrap.

there will be certain areas where the tension is too intense for the vinyl to hold if you attempt to wrap them with one single piece, which may cause it to lift and fail over time.

Usually, this is an area that contains a deep or drastic recess, and typically these areas are found at the front and rear bumpers and around the grille, fog lights, and rear license plate area. To alleviate these high-tension areas, plan on laying pieces of vinyl inside these areas prior to laying the entire panel in question.

These pieces are commonly referred to as inlays. If done correctly, they will look inconspicuous and (at the same time) eliminate unwanted tension that may cause the wrap to lift and fail. Plan ahead of time where the appropriate places to put these inlays will be.

Use your knifeless tape and follow the natural body lines of the vehicle that allow you to make them much less noticeable to the average viewer. Inlays are common on a full wrap. They ensure longevity and eliminate any potential issues that the wrap may have when trying to hold in tight places. It is the highly skilled installer who knows when and where to use them and to keep them as hidden as possible. The more practice you have at using them, the better you will become at applying them.

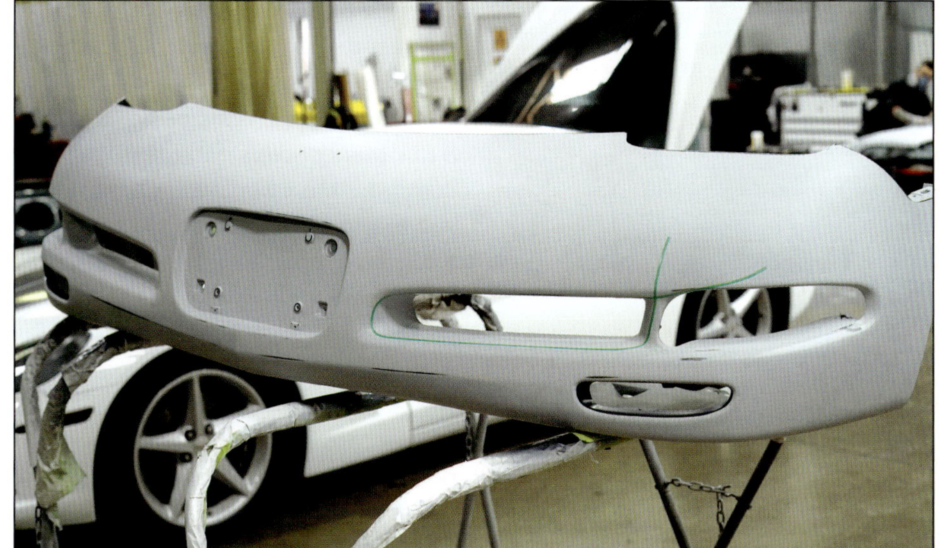

This bumper was taken from a 2004 C5 Corvette. Since it is an older vehicle, it was sanded, primed, and prepped to ensure that no flaws are present before the wrap is applied. Our first step is to lay the vinyl inside the areas where the wrap will be under the most amount of tension. These inlays decrease the tension and increase the longevity of the wrap.

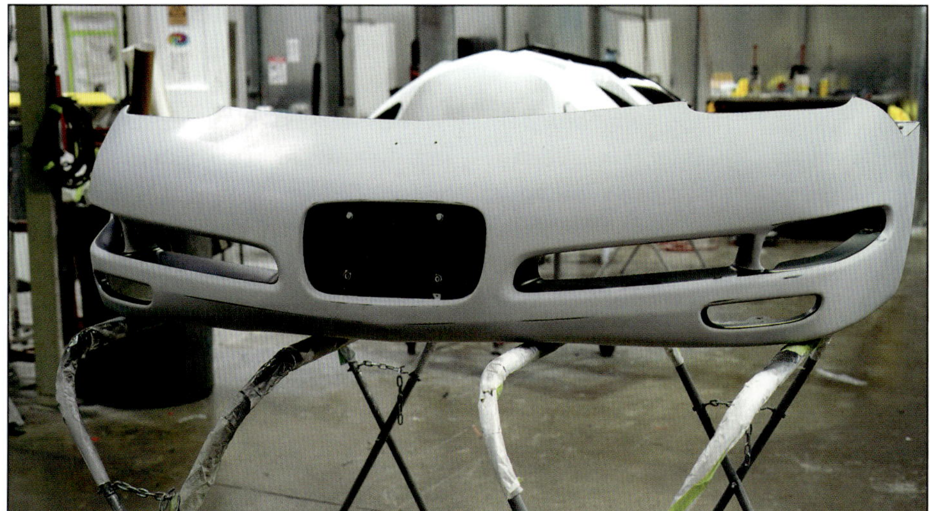

Here is the full bumper with all the inlays installed. Notice how we have determined (after close examination) which areas the vinyl is under the most stress, and we eliminated each one by using an inlay.

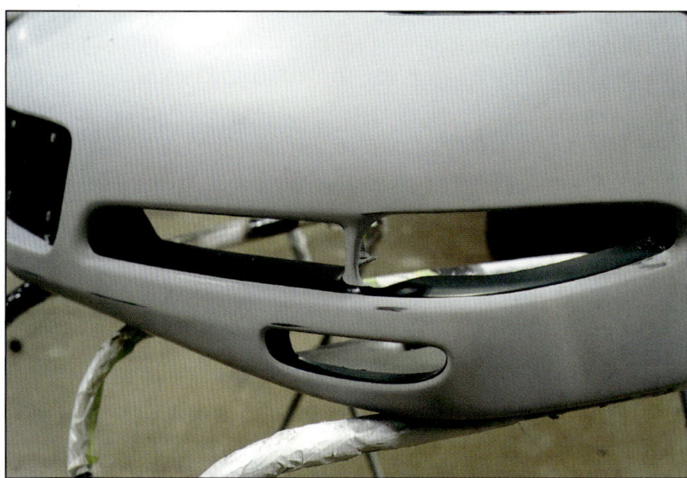

This is a close-up of a few areas where inlays are used to eliminate high-tension areas.

The green knifeless tape has been applied prior to installing the inlay.

Here is a photo of the same bumper after it has been wrapped but prior to installing the plastic inserts and fog lights. As long as the knifeless tape was nice and straight when the inlays were made, the seams will look clean and go virtually unnoticed.

Once all of the inlays are installed, the rest of the bumper is ready to be wrapped. Do not to fully install the bumper onto the vehicle—just tighten a few bolts or clips enough to get it sturdy for the installation because you may want to remove the bumper after the wrap installation to make the edges clean.

Seams

Another great skill to have in your arsenal is the ability to create a clean-looking seam. There are various situations where it is beneficial to incorporate a seam into a panel or section. Usually when you encounter a panel that is greater than 60 inches in both directions, your only option is to seam two pieces of vinyl together to cover the entire panel. You will often find yourself in this situation when wrapping classic cars, as the hood, roof, and trunk areas are larger than most modern vehicles.

When wrapping horizontal panels like these, use your knifeless tape to follow an existing body line to help disguise the seam. In some cases, a natural body line is not present, so you need to measure to find the middle line of the panel and lay your seam as straight as possible to give it a clean look. Other panels that may require a seam are found on some larger types of modern vehicles, such as the Ford Raptor. Here you will find that when you measure the cab area, the height and width of the cab are both greater than 60 inches. However, in this case, you are wrapping a vertical panel so the seam is easier to hide.

Along the bottom of each door is a natural indention located approxi-mately 15 inches above the bottom of the doors that runs the entire length of the cab. This is a perfect place to position the seam, as it is virtually invisible to the average viewer. It is important to install the vinyl starting with the lower piece first. When it's allowable, build your panel from the bottom up. By laying the bottom piece first, it will allow the top piece to lay over it, which will place the seam facing downward. This makes the seam less obvious and a lot less noticeable than if you were to lay your top piece first with the bottom piece over it.

Side Mirrors

Side mirrors are some of the most difficult parts of a car to master when it comes to wrapping. These are sections of the vehicle that tend to lift and fail the most. If these sections are going to fail, they will usually do so within the first few weeks of being out on the road and exposed to the elements.

There are several tricks and techniques to decrease the chances of these areas of the car from failing. In the chapters to come, we will teach you how to recognize these areas prior to installation and how to use strategic techniques (such as incorporating seams, applying heat with an infrared lamp, and stretching the material correctly) to keep your mirrors free from lifting and look great for the lifetime of the wrap.

INSTALLATION PREPARATION

Now that we've discussed the importance of a clean work environment, we can address vehicle preparation for the work at hand.

As with any quality project, the result hinges on preparation. Any bodywork specialist will say that a paint job will never be right without countless amounts of hours of prep. Set yourself up for success when vinyl wrapping a vehicle. Use an organized workspace; a clean, perfect surface; and move as many unnecessary items out of your way as possible to apply the vinyl.

Preparing the Work Area

Having the proper tools and equipment available is imperative to prepare your work area. Be sure to have the tools that were discussed in Chapter 5 at your disposal. Bridging a panel (leaving the stretched film exposed from one panel to another waiting to be cut back) is not ideal while you are running off to the store to buy a tool.

If you're working with your own vehicle, you will know the current condition of the paint and how you need to prepare for your project. If you are working on a client or friend's car, it is important to have many items available to address paint issues. This can include a simple cleaning and clay bar all the way to intense body repairs that require specialty body tools.

Old Vinyl Removal

There are a variety of films on the market today. Even in some brand lines, some adhesives separate easier than others. In addition, various colors absorb sunlight differently, and therefore the amount of work required for a removal can vary. With any type of removal, try a small area of the car first and then go on to the rest after a test is successfully completed.

Chemical Removal

Several products are on the market for chemically removing vinyl.

A paint booth works well to wrap a vehicle. With paint, a perfectly controlled environment is needed because as a speck of dust can ruin hours of prep work. Filters, ventilation, and lighting are all ideal for vehicle wraps as well. Get the environment for a wrap as clean and well-lit as possible.

A product that we often use is Rapid Remover, which can be purchased through the company Fellers in most states. Rapid Remover can be applied on the outside of the installed vinyl and removed. It works by activating the adhesive and softening the film.

Much of the vinyl can be removed by using Rapid Remover, but it may leave some adhesive residue on the paint. The residue removal is usually not too extensive when vinyl is chemically removed.

Chemical removals can make difficult removal jobs more bearable. However, be careful about what products you use. As always, perform a test in a small spot on the vehicle before taking on the entire job.

Chemical removers are not always without trouble. They can be messy, and, depending on the vinyl status, they can cause you more work instead of less. It is best to leave a chemical removal only for the most difficult removals.

Heat Removal

In warm environments, the sun can be the best tool for removing vinyl. The sun will heat the adhesive and allow it to be removed from the panel. This technique counts on a few assumptions: the film is of high quality and it is being removed within its life span. If these criteria are not met, you can be in for quite the ride.

Problematic removals often look white no matter what the original color. The white is basically the pigment burning out of the vinyl. Worse than fading, the telltale sign that you're in for a miserable removal is if the film looks cracked. We've spent many days removing vinyl that is well past its life at the cost of the skin on our fingertips.

Films in good condition still take some elbow grease to remove, but they are not nearly the nightmare of pulling off thousands of little pieces. Wrap should come off in full panels just like it was applied to the vehicle.

After a removal is completed, any residue that is left over can be removed with 3M 08984 General Purpose Adhesive Cleaner, which is available at most auto parts suppliers. This product should be tested in an inconspicuous area before it is used on the entire vehicle. As you will quickly see, it does an incredible job of removing any leftover adhesive from the vehicle.

Adhesive remover should not be left for long periods of time on the paint or vinyl. Installers in shops quite often make the mistake of leaving a rag full of adhesive remover on a vinyl-wrapped or painted surface. Do not do this! Put your tools away at the completion of any project, especially any tools soaked in chemicals.

Removing Old Vinyl Wrap

1 *This wrap has outlived its usefulness. It was originally a satin black hood wrap that is now white and is showing a lot of wear. First, a vinyl wrap becomes dull; then, it whitens and cracks. Wraps are easy to remove when they're pristine, but they can be difficult at this stage. When they get to the cracking stage, it can be too late to save the paint. A little corner piece has been pulled off here. At this stage, the wrap will be difficult to remove; it will come off in tiny bits.*

1a *Rapid Remover and the trash bag technique were used to remove this wrap. The bag keeps the moisture from drying immediately, and Rapid Remover loosens the adhesive on the film to allow for easier removal.*

1b *Rapid Remover was applied using a squirt bottle. Then, the vehicle was wrapped with trash bags and taped down. The sun is helpful to speed up the process. Be careful that the remover does not dry out the Rapid Remover too quickly. Usually about 10 to 15 minutes is enough time to loosen the film, but it depends on the outdoor heat. Test the film by pulling back the trash bag, grab an edge of the vinyl, and then start to pull back. If the vinyl is still brittle, it's not ready. If the vinyl pulls off, remove as much as you can. Sometimes it is necessary to respray and tape the trash bags down and try again. Repeat this until all the vinyl is removed.*

2 *Check to see if the film is ready to be removed.*

2a *The film comes off much easier with the Rapid Remover. It will come off in larger pieces and almost looks as if it has its color back. It still takes some work due to how long the film was left on the vehicle, but it is still much easier than without Rapid Remover.*

3 *All the film is now removed. There may or may not be a slight haziness on the paint. This is the leftover adhesive. Since vinyl is layered, the adhesive can separate from the outer layer, especially in older films. When you run your hand across the surface, it will feel rough. Don't leave the car this way.*

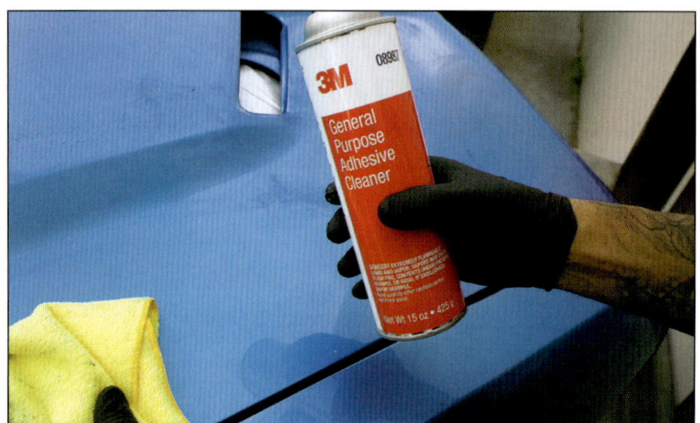

4 *The 3M 08987 adhesive remover works wonders on adhesive removal. The leftover glue residue is visible in the picture. Use a microfiber cloth with the remover, and with a bit of work, the adhesive can be removed. If you get to the point where you are just spreading the adhesive around, you need a new cloth. It is important to not leave adhesive-soaked rags on paint or vinyl because it will deteriorate the surface. Wash the car with soap and water when the adhesive is removed. Always test your products in a subtle area of the vehicle before any project.*

4a *Some prefer 3M's remover, but some use Rapid Remover. Whatever your choice, it is necessary to remove residue such as this. Soap and water will not do the job. On stubborn items, such as a sign where the paint is not important, a plastic razor blade can be used to help with residue removal. Do not use this on vehicle paint!*

Body Repairs

For information on bodywork repair, pick up a copy of CarTech's *Automotive Bodywork & Rust Repair* by Matt Joseph to learn what is needed to prep the vehicle's surface.

This book is about vehicle wraps, and for the most part, we assume that you have a perfect surface with which to work. So, you are applying vinyl to a new or almost new vehicle without major body issues.

Another warning is if the surface looks amazing because it was recently painted, we highly advise waiting at least a few months for the paint cure process to be completed. The adhesives of proper vinyl films are so strong that they can rip up aftermarket paint when the vinyl is removed. This may not always affect the initial install if the film is not repositioned much, but it can cause damage when it is removed years later. High-end vinyl films are made to be applied to OEM paint surfaces; anything else is taking a risk.

If you have some light surface defects, they should be prepped with 400- to 600-grit sandpaper by hand or with a dual-action sander. If body-filler work is done on a panel before a vinyl wrap, always have a protective layer of primer over the filler work.

Many people think that vinyl is enough of a protective layer over filler work, but that is not the case. Vinyl breathes, which allows air and moisture to seep into the existing body filler work under the wrap. When this happens, it creates a mapping effect, and all the spots of bodywork will swell or contract and cause the bodywork to stand out like a sore thumb.

Body Parts Removal

Just like a paint job, we highly advise removing interfering body parts from the vehicle to ensure the best possible result for the wrap. In the early years, people wrapped around and over just about anything. Later, people realized that if they prep a wrap like a paint job, a showroom-type look can be attained.

The most common items that get in the way are door handles, lights, roof racks, and emblems, but all vehicles are different. On some vehicles, you are better off leaving some items installed if you can get around them. Seams are your enemy.

This Corvette has been keyed in several places. Before it is wrapped, the body issues from the paint damage need to be addressed. Several areas have been sanded down. If you can feel any roughness with your fingers, it will be seen in the wrap. We have clay barred the vehicle to have the best and smoothest surface possible.

Creating a guide template can help with reinstalling emblem letters. Before the emblem is removed, take a piece of tape and mark out the start and end of each letter. This will provide a measurement for spacing. Make sure your tape line is straight, and it will act as a guide for making the emblem level.

By using the template as a guide, we can install the new black lettering. Black is popular for emblems. Many emblems are available in black and can be purchased online or at some vehicle dealer parts departments. The other option is to paint the emblem black. If you paint them, the original or a new emblem can be used. Always use a new adhesive backing if an emblem is reused.

So, if not removing an item is going to cause you to patch in vinyl, you should remove it.

It is nearly impossible to walk through how to remove every item on every vehicle, so we suggest searching YouTube or OEM walk-throughs for guidance on how to dismantle vehicles. Don't be like the people who used to wrap over or around items in the early days. If quality is paramount to you, remove parts from the vehicle.

Emblems can be expensive. There are several products on the market to reattach emblems when the project is completed. These can be purchased from your local paint supply store. There are glues, double-stick tapes, etc. for reapplying emblems, but we highly suggest buying new emblems with fresh adhesive. Not only is it the best possible look but it also keeps you from accidentally ruining your wrap with glue or some unruly double-sided tape.

Many of our installers build templates of the badge's position on the car before removal. This helps as a guide for reinstalling the badges. Using tape lines or templates can help position the emblems in the right spot.

One last popular option is called a debadge. This is where you remove the badge and leave it off. You're removing the badge for the wrap anyway. Many people like the look of no significant branding.

Vehicle Surface Cleaning

Wraps do not hide imperfections. They do not hide paint issues, and they certainly do not hide dirt and grime. One speck of dust can look like a pimple under your perfect wrap. Washing and prepping the vehicle before the wrap is an absolute necessity. Wrapping a vehicle is a lot of work. Do not see the work go to waste by not being careful from the start.

Soap and Water

Wash and clean to remove any major debris or bug guts from the vehicle. This is no different than a general car wash. If you're being hired to wrap a car, ask the owner to wash the car vehicle before the appointment. Even if you need to go over it again, the major dirt and grime will be gone and save some time.

Standard car-wash soaps that leave no residue are ideal for this first wash. Advise the client not to use any soap with wax because it can affect the adhesive on the wrap and make installation difficult.

Also, advise against tire shine. People load up tires with this stuff, and it gets flung all over the finished wrap. Tire shine will not completely ruin most wraps if it is addressed quickly, but it's also not something you want on it.

Degreaser

The first step after the car wash but before the wrap is to degrease. Using a standard degreasing solution, such as 409, dilute the degreaser to 2/3 water and 1/3 degreaser. Spray the solution on each panel of the vehicle and wipe it with a microfiber cloth. The yellow microfiber cloths from Costco are among the best we've found.

All areas of the vehicle that will be wrapped must go through this step to avoid any contaminants under the film. This should be done just prior to the alcohol mix.

Alcohol Mix

The last step of prep before the vinyl application is to spray on the isopropyl alcohol solution and then wipe it off with a clean rag. Use a mixture of 65 to 70 percent isopropyl alcohol and 30 to 35 percent water. Remember to wear latex gloves when dealing with isopropyl alcohol, which can be found at almost any grocery or hardware store or large chemical supplier.

INSTALLATION TECHNIQUES

It's time to start laying some vinyl onto the vehicle. Installing the vinyl is the most rewarding part of the whole process, and this chapter gives you the tips necessary to make the process as enjoyable as possible.

By using the techniques discussed in this chapter, you can reduce the total installation time and avoid time-consuming mistakes. We will begin with measuring tips and tricks and end with a few stretching maneuvers.

We've measured the car and added 6 additional inches to each side. This eliminates the headache of cutting the material too close and decreases the odds of making a mistake.

Measurements

Taking measurements can be time consuming, even more so if you go panel by panel. The first instinct as an installer may be to measure a panel, cut it off the roll, and install it. You will spend a lot of time going back and forth to the vehicle doing it this way.

Instead, make a list of measurements for every panel of the vehicle before you begin cutting and wrapping. Doing it this way can save a lot of time in the long run.

People often try to save material by shortening the dimensions. This will do more harm than good. Add a good 6 inches of film on all four sides when the measurements are recorded. There is no reason to make a panel more difficult to install just to save a few inches of material.

Film Cutting

With all the measurements recorded, take a quick overview of all the measured panels. Keep in

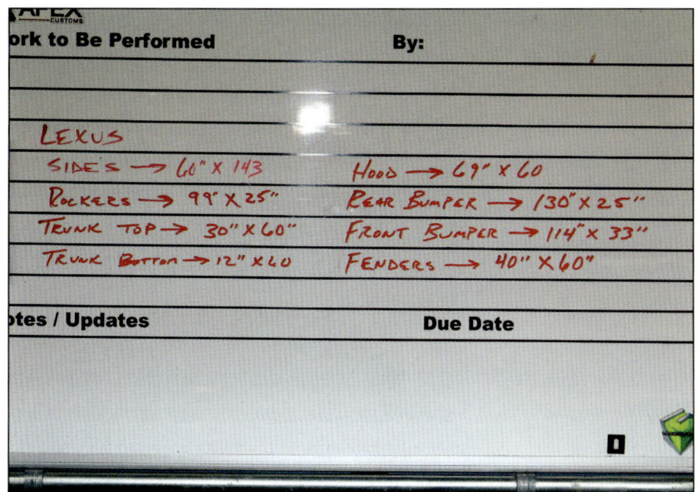

Measuring every panel at the beginning is a real time saver. I record my measurements on a dry erase board, take a photo of it with my cell phone, and then take my phone to the cut table to begin cutting all the panels.

Record the measurements for every panel that will be wrapped. Before cutting, remember this rule: measure three times, cut once.

Cutting and labeling all panels at once is a massive time saver. Once all the panels have been cut, place them inside the vehicle. It is convenient to reach inside the vehicle and begin a new panel.

mind that the width of the roll is 60 inches. Look for panels that can be combined and cut next to each other on the roll. This will help get the most panels out of the amount of film.

For example, the front and rear bumpers of the vehicle are usually be around 30 inches tall. Even if the front bumper is 34 inches tall, check to see if 26 inches will be enough for the rear. Getting two bumpers out of one 60-inch piece of vinyl is always a big win.

Since you wrote down all of the vehicle's panel dimensions beforehand, it is much easier to figure out which panels can be combined like this.

Look at the model of the vehicle that is about to be wrapped and plan ahead of time how each panel will go down. Pay special attention to the sides of the vehicle. For example, examine the rocker panel below the doors. Does it connect to the rear

quarter panel? If so, consider wrapping the door(s) and rocker and rear quarter panels with one big piece of vinyl instead of separate pieces. This is another way to save material. We do this with most of our full color changes.

Now that you have the measurements and a good idea of how each panel will go on the vehicle, it is time to cut the film. After years of experience, we prefer to cut all the panels at once. We typically put them all inside the vehicle so we can wrap a panel and move on to the next one without having to leave the work area. Doing it this way greatly increases the efficiency of the installation.

If you choose to use the same process, label every panel so that you do not mix them up. Cutting every panel before the wrap will also provide a good idea of how much material there is on hand and whether you need to order more, which allows for time to do so.

Heat Application

Using controlled temperatures during installation is essential when wrapping a vehicle. Your environment should never be too far above or below normal room temperature. Working in an environment that is too hot, such as above 80°F, can cause the material to become too soft. An area with the temperature below 75°F can cause the film to become stiff and brittle. This may cause the film to snap and break whenever the installer needs to pull on it during the install.

Films with a matte finish are notorious for breaking under conditions that are too cold. An ideal environment is one that is indoors and clean with a controlled temperature between 75 and 80°F. Installing vinyl wrap film outdoors is not recommended, but there may be times when it is your only option. In these cases, be prepared. Plan and check the weather forecast so that you can schedule the project accordingly.

Let's discuss how and when to apply heat while installing panels.

TECH TIP

Allow for Extra Material

Give yourself at least an extra 6 inches when measuring the panels. It does not pay to try and save material here. A panel that has been cut with plenty of material to spare is much easier to install. ■

Burning Vinyl with Propane and a Heat Gun

We do not recommend using propane to heat your vinyl. The intense heat can create a mistake quickly. In addition, keep your heat gun moving at all times. Concentrated heat in a singular area will result in an unwelcomed blemish.

This is an unheated section of 3M 2080 Deep Matte Black. We will demonstrate how overheating the vinyl with a propane torch can damage the material and require replacement of the panel.

When using a propane torch, overheating can occur quickly without warning.

Even though they are easy to carry and portable, it is not recommended to use a propane torch on material used in full color changes. The flame will heat the material quickly and has the potential to damage the vinyl. These propane torches are better suited for commercial installations.

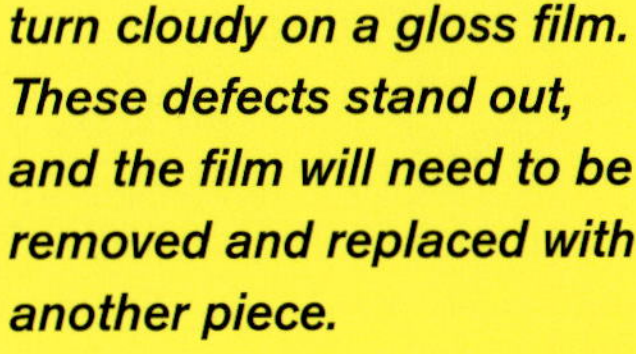

When a material with a matte or satin finish has been heated past its threshold, it will glaze in that area and give it a shiny appearance. The material needs to be discarded when this happens. The area will turn cloudy on a gloss film. These defects stand out, and the film will need to be removed and replaced with another piece.

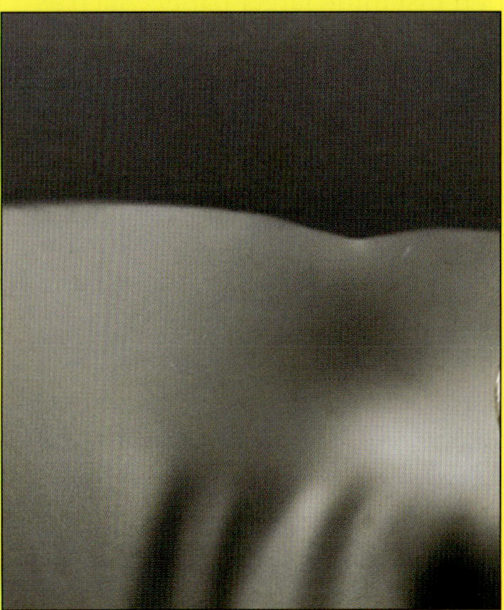

Heating the vinyl with a heat gun rather than a torch is a much safer alternative. The time that it takes to create a heat distortion mark is much longer when using a gun.

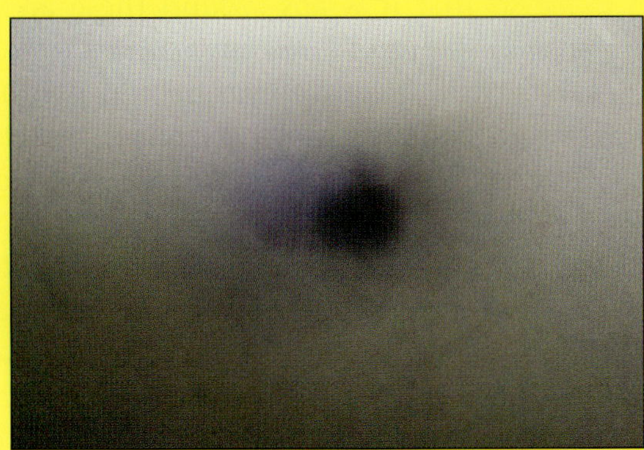

Although it is less likely, damage from a heat gun still can occur. Wave the nose of the gun in a circular motion to evenly apply heat to the vinyl. Never leave a heat gun focused on one area of the vinyl for a long period of time.

Almost all vinyl wrap film is designed where heat can be applied to its exterior surface once the backing has been removed. Doing so will make the vinyl softer, more pliable, and allow it to be stretched. Flat panels, such as roofs and hoods, can usually be installed using little heat. However, panels that have bends and curves, such as fenders, bumpers, and trunks, will need to be heated as the installer is laying the panel.

Heat Gun and Heat Lamp

Two main tools are used when applying heat to the vinyl: a heat gun and an infrared heating lamp. A heat gun is highly portable and easy to use while heating smaller panels. An infrared heating lamp is preferred when installing larger panels, such as trunks and bumpers.

Many installers also incorporate the use of a propane torch. Although it can be handy due to its mobility and smaller size, beginners should not use it. Novice installers will discover that the heat coming off the torch gets hot extremely fast and can easily create heat distortion marks on the surface of the vinyl that are permanent and will force the installer to replace the panel. Only use a propane torch for commercial installs where the laminate that covers the vinyl is much thicker and will not be damaged as easily.

Horizontal Stretch

The most important method to learn when installing a vinyl wrap on any vehicle is horizontal stretch. We often tell our students that once they fully understand this concept, they will not only see the quality of their wraps increase dramatically but it will also greatly reduce the amount

Propane torches are recommended when installing commercial wraps. When using a propane torch, keep the tip of the flame approximately 6 to 8 inches away from the surface of the vehicle. Always keep the flame moving and never heat a specific area for more than a few seconds.

The apex of the fender panel protrudes outward just above the wheel well area. There is a natural recess to either side of the area. It is important to give the material the right amount of horizontal stretch when laying the film to give a smooth appearance as seen here. This will speed up your install and make the installation less difficult.

of time it takes to finish a panel. These qualities will help transform an amateur wrapper into a professional installer.

Heating and Pulling

First, when wrapping a curved panel, it is important to notice that the material will naturally be tight and smooth along the apex, which is the area of the curve that protrudes outward the most. Portions of the material that have not been heated or stretched enough around these areas will have a buildup of excess material. This is exactly what you do not want. It is extremely difficult to install

smoothly when it comes time to apply it with a squeegee, and it is much more susceptible to lifting. It is highly likely to fail after it is exposed to the sun.

The key is to install the vinyl so that it wraps around these areas smoothly. To accomplish this, use a combination of heating and pulling to complete the horizontal stretch. Most vinyl material, when heated, can be stretched to increase its original size by approximately 15 to 20 percent. Note that once the material has been stretched and given time to cool, it can shrink back to its original size by reapplying heat if the vinyl is loose and not under any tension.

The vinyl laid over the recessed areas has not been stretched properly and resulted in a buildup of excess material. Installing a panel like this will take more time and be more difficult.

When wrapping a panel with recesses, remember that a piece that has been heated and stretched over a recess will be much more vulnerable to heat.

Material that is stretched over a recess will burn rapidly. It will only take a few seconds to burn a hole through the vinyl.

Unfortunately, the installer must replace this panel.

If a panel is installed loosely and without the appropriate amount of stretch, it may require more adjustments and time to complete.

Never heat and stretch at the same time; it may damage the vinyl. It is also important that you never heat a portion of the material that has been stretched over a recess and is floating above the vehicle's surface. The vinyl stretched over these areas is under a significant amount of tension, and a small amount of heat can easily burn a hole right through the vinyl.

Horizontal Stretch Technique

Now that we have established what not to do, let's begin by executing the horizontal stretch technique while installing a front fender panel. Fenders are usually the friendliest of panels when it comes to curvature, but the angle of a Corvette fender or the roundness of a Porsche fender can pose some challenges. Thank-fully, with the use of the horizontal stretch, the panel can be a lot easier to install.

First, the piece of material should be about 6 or 7 inches taller than the actual panel. The length of many fenders from the door to the head-light area is less than 60 inches, which is the typical width of a vinyl roll, so it will not result in a lot of material waste to cut your panel nice and tall. If you try to wrap the fender to where you only have an inch or two to spare as it goes over the top and toward the hood area, you might experience some high tension during installation that could lead to what is referred to as "fingering" and ulti-mately cause some lifting.

Laying Vinyl on a Fender

1 *All obstructions have been removed from the passenger side fender. The surface has been thoroughly cleaned and prepped, which makes the vinyl ready to be applied.*

2 *Using a two-person installation system, one person stands adjacent to the door with the other person standing near the front of the car.*

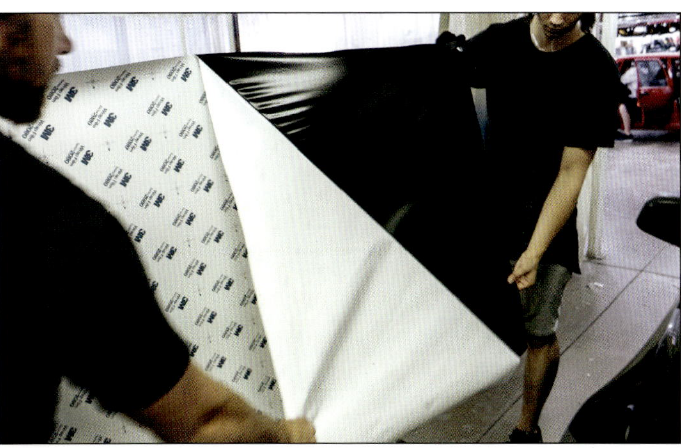

3 *With the vinyl adhesive side facing the car, take one last visual check to ensure that everything is aligned and ready for application.*

4 *While holding the piece high above the ground to avoid contamination, peel the backing from the material. Keep the material tight so that the wrap doesn't fold onto itself.*

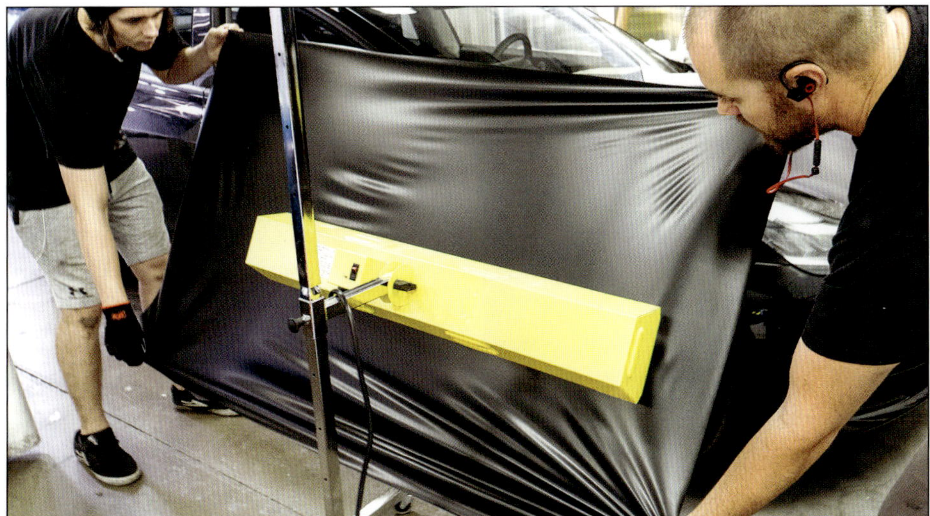

5 *With the backing fully removed, place the vinyl approximately 12 inches in front of a heat lamp and slowly move the material until the entire panel is heated. The distance between the heat lamp and vehicle should be about 2 feet.*

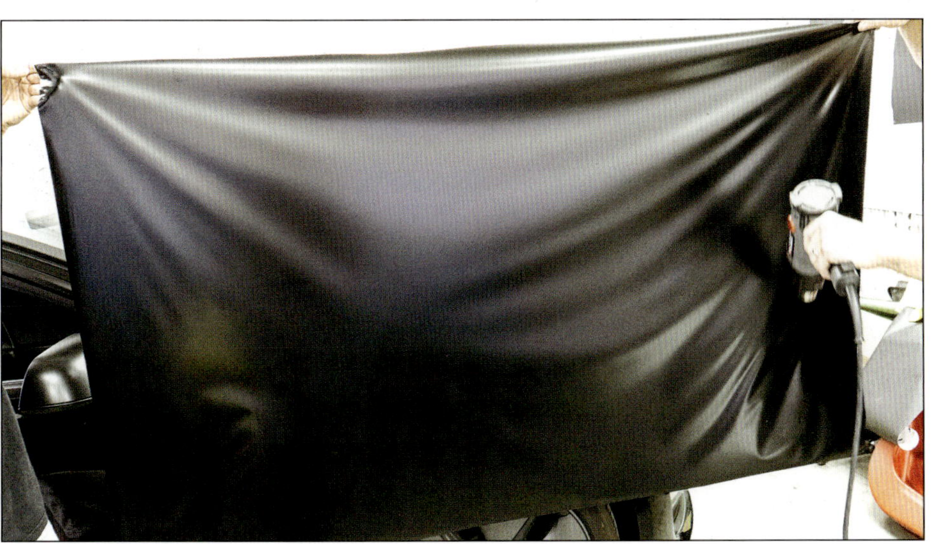

6 *If an infrared heat lamp is not available, the same effect can be accomplished with a heat gun. Although this may take more time, the material will eventually reach the temperature necessary for installation.*

7 *The right side of the material has been heated, and the section on the left has not. Pass the gun to the second installer and have them heat the area. As the entire section is heated, the vinyl will become much softer. When this occurs, the vinyl is ready to be laid.*

8 *Walk up to the panel and stretch the piece while it hovers a few inches above the vehicle.*

9 *As soon as the stretch has been applied by both installers, press the vinyl against the fender and continue to lay the piece onto the surface of the vehicle.*

10 *When done successfully, the vinyl will cover the entire section of the panel with a few extra inches to spare on all four sides. The material should be stretched and have a smooth appearance that is almost entirely free of wrinkles. A panel that looks like this photo its initial lay is one that can be completed quickly.*

Once you are happy with the size of the material, have one installer stand at the headlight area and the other installer positioned at the area where the door begins. This all takes place immediately after the cleaning phase. While holding the material high above the ground (to prevent any dust from contaminating the exposed adhesive side of the vinyl) and using tension between the two installers, pull and remove the protective backing from the vinyl.

Once the backing has been removed, apply heat to the vinyl's exterior. I prefer to use the infrared heating lamp. Not only does it heat a larger surface of the material at once, it's also hands free and allows both installers to hold all four corners of the material. If you do not have access to a lamp, use a heat gun by using one hand to hold the top corner of the vinyl and the other to heat the material while passing the gun to the other installer.

As the temperature of the material increases, you will visually see it getting softer and notice which areas are ready and which ones require more heat. Glance at the fender and take notice as to where the curves and bends are on the vehicle. These are the areas you want to heat last, so they are nice and warm when laying the material onto the vehicle.

Laying Vinyl on a Panel

Now that the vinyl has been heated, both installers will immediately step toward the panel being laid. The material only takes a few seconds to cool, so move quickly. The next few steps are crucial to execute this technique successfully.

As you both approach the vehicle with your heated material, make sure it is positioned in a way that provides plenty of coverage on all four sides of the panel. Vocally confirm this with your installation partner and make sure there is plenty of material on their end. Time is of the essence, so do this as quickly as possible.

Hover the material to where it is only a few inches away from making contact with the surface of the panel. The goal is to get the material close to the surface without making contact. If one installer accidentally touches the car with the film, reheat the material and start again.

Stretch the Vinyl

With the film hovering slightly above the surface, the next step is to stretch the vinyl. Again, communicate with the other installer so that both of you are aware it is time to stretch. If you start to pull without notifying your partner, you risk pulling the material right out of their hands.

Gently pull the vinyl horizontally while bringing the material to the surface of the panel and contacting the vehicle. Keep in mind that there is a limit to how far the material can be stretched, and overstretching the film can produce defects in the finish and cause color distortion. It takes a little practice to master this technique, but it helps to remember that the pull and the stretch happens just before contacting the vehicle, not after. When done correctly, you have a nice smooth surface with the vinyl securely covering all four edges of the fender.

You have now completed the horizontal stretch technique and are ready to begin applying the vinyl to the surface with your squeegee. If there is one thing to take away from this section of the book, it is to know that your initial lay of each panel of the vehicle is one of the most crucial steps to a successful wrap. It is the one step that, if done correctly, has the potential to make every other step that follows it a whole lot easier. Using the horizontal stretch technique and mastering the initial lay of every panel of the vehicle will put you well on your way to becoming a professional vinyl wrap installer.

Apply Pressure

Immediately following the initial lay, the next step in the installation process is to apply pressure to the film using the squeegee tool until the entire panel is adhered to the vehicle. Due to the complexity and importance of this step, we go into detail on how it is performed in Chapter 9. For now, we will assume the panel has been fully adhered to the surface and proceed to the following step, which is trimming and cutting the panel.

Trimming

Once the panel has been laid and the film has been squeegeed onto the surface of the vehicle, it is time to trim and cut out the panel. I have always used a metal Olfa knife loaded with replaceable stainless-steel breakaway blades. I always keep it in the same back pocket so that I know exactly where to find it.

This is an ultrasharp carbon blade and pack of 50 replacement blades.

These carbon blades are so sharp that they are capable of etching glass. Novice installers are not recommended to use this type of blade.

Most of the cuts will be worry-free without any potential of your blade making contact with the surface area of the vehicle. To do this, create what installers to refer to as a "bridge."

Blade Pressure

There are times where a small portion of the cutting requires you to cut vinyl that is placed over painted areas. In these cases, it is all about applying just the right amount of pressure softly with the blade to where it only cuts through the vinyl and not the surface below it. The only way to achieve this is through experience.

As a beginner, you never want to attempt this until you have practiced and are comfortable with your cutting technique. To do this, acquire some scrap material with a variety of finishes. A satin, gloss, and matte material is a good mix. Each one has a slightly different feel. Find a practice surface that you can lay the vinyl on. Begin by making numerous cuts in a straight line. Start softly, and gradually increase pressure until you discover how much is required to cut through the material. Remove the vinyl and examine the area for cuts on the surface. Repeat this until you feel comfortable cutting in a straight line.

Practice making lines that are curved. It seems strange, but most people will naturally apply more pressure when creating a curved line with a blade. Make multiple cuts and continue to check underneath the vinyl for damage. You will soon become familiar with just how hard to press.

Remember to snap off the tip of the blade after a few cuts. This might sound strange, but there is a greater potential of damaging paint with a dull blade because it forces you to use too much pressure as you try to get through the material. ■

Creating a Bridge

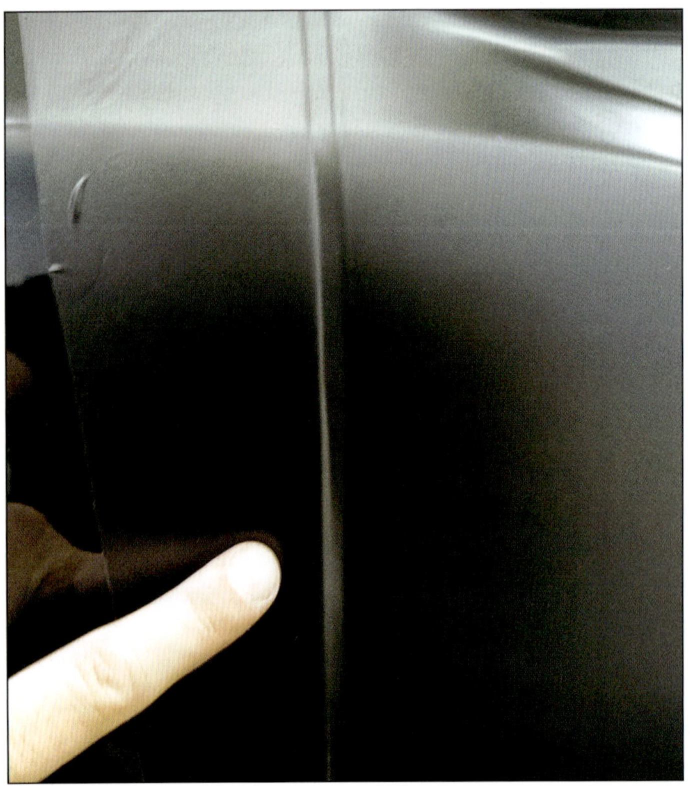

1 *This is what vinyl installers refer to as a bridge. This offers a free space to cut through the film without the blade making contact with the panel.*

1a *This wrap glove is manufactured by Avery Dennison and allows the installer to apply pressure to the vinyl without any resistance.*

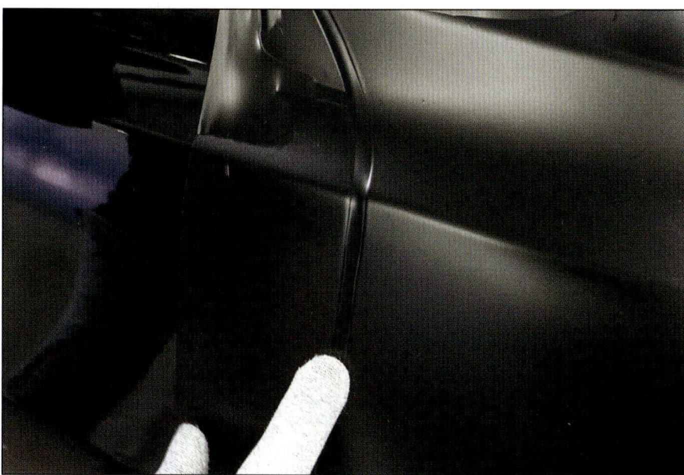

1b *While wearing a wrap glove, press firmly along both edges of the panels with your finger and follow downward to create a perfect bridge.*

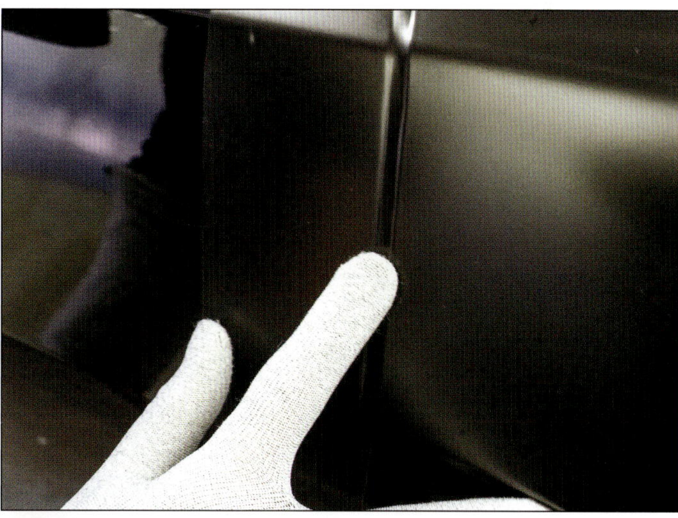

2 *Make the cut along the edge farthest from the panel that was just installed.*

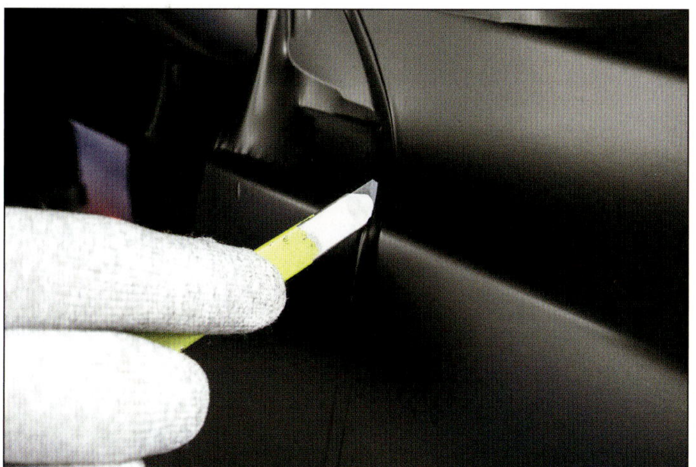

2a *Insert the tip of the blade into the bridge.*

2b *The edge of the neighboring panel will act as a guide when the panel is being cut.*

Bridge

Creating a bridge is done by placing the material past the panel you are currently wrapping and placing it at least a few inches onto a neighboring panel. Put on a wrap glove when the panel has been laid and before you begin cutting. Gloves like these are made from a slick material that allows you to run your hand or finger along the surface of material with a much lower resistance than if you used your bare hand.

After the bridge is created, run your finger over the length of the bridge to ensure that the material is firmly pressed down on both sides. This provides the proper amount of tension that is needed to make the cut, and it provides a good visual to let you know where to place the blade.

Take out your knife and snap off the top section of the blade. Get used to doing this before every new cut. Starting at one end of the bridge, insert the tip of the blade to where its side is resting against the edge of the neighboring panel. That edge will act as your guide as you follow it down, and you'll eventually cut the entire length of the bridge. Repeat the process on the remaining three sides to complete the panel.

Tucking

In areas that do not feature a natural gap, such as around some headlamp areas, use the "lift and tuck" method. It is necessary to use this technique to ensure that the entire surface of the factory painted surface is covered. A quality color change will almost always have every inch of the original paint hidden.

Notice the area between the fender panel and the headlamp. An installer will often encounter a gap that is too narrow to successfully execute a bridge approach. In this case, the correct method requires lifting and tucking the material before the cut is made.

Tucking Vinyl Wrap

1 *After the panel has been laid, make a relief cut along the length of the headlamp to give the installer a few inches of loose material to hold onto.*

2 *Pop the material off the headlamp until there is no tension on the vinyl where the gap lies between the panel and the headlamp.*

3 *With all the tension released, use the hard edge of the squeegee and begin tucking in the vinyl. Begin at the top of the headlamp.*

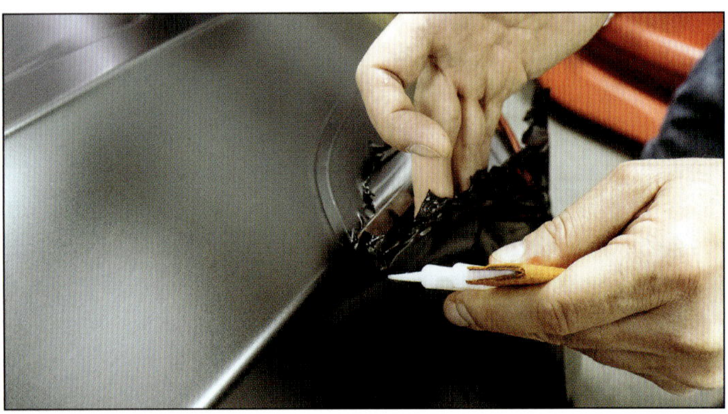

4 *Follow the contour downward to ensure the tuck will be firm.*

5 *Finish the lift and tuck method by completing the tuck at the bottom of the light.*

To accomplish this, lift the edge of the material that rides against a tight area of the vehicle. While using the hard edge of a squeegee, tuck it into that area. Make sure that there isn't any trapped air in this area. Once this is confirmed, begin to run the tip of the blade along the area to complete the cut. When making cuts to a panel, it is often less time consuming to complete them all before moving on to the next step, which is tucking the vinyl.

Cutting Excess Vinyl around the Tuck

1 *When the tucking has been completed, begin the cut.*

2 *Insert the tip of the blade along the outer edge of the panel and gently rest the side of the blade against the headlamp.*

3 *Use the edge of the lamp as a guide and continue cutting downward toward the bottom of the lamp.*

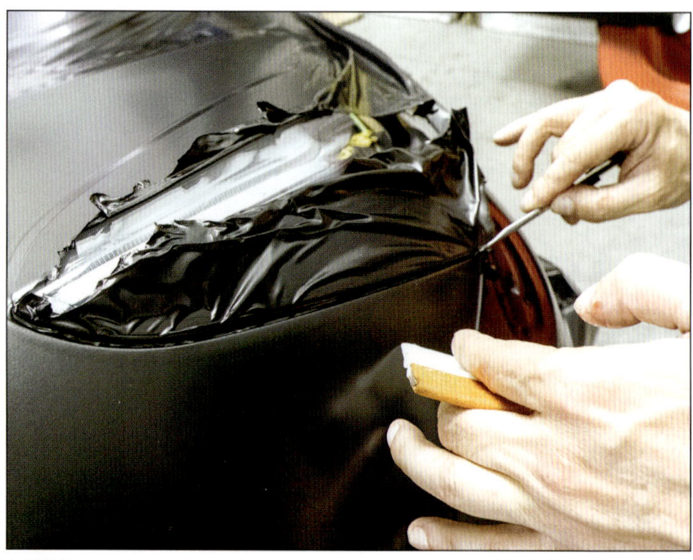

4 *Complete the cut after using the lift-and-tuck method.*

5 *Remove the excess vinyl from the headlamp.*

6 *Now that the vinyl has been removed, use the hard edge of the squeegee and firmly tuck the rest of the vinyl.*

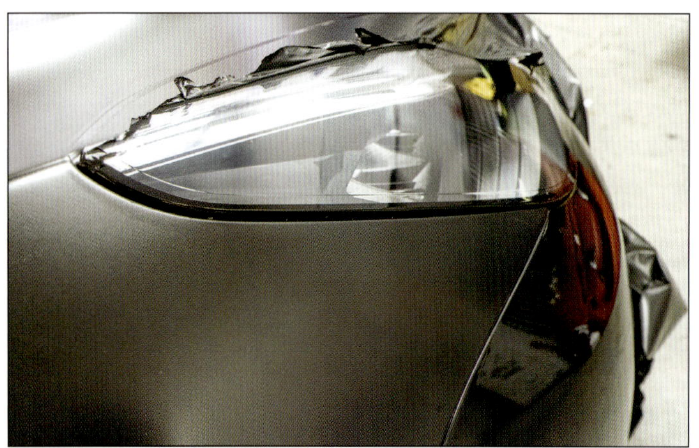

7 *The panel after the cut and tuck has been completed.*

This is the top area of the passenger-side fender after the cut was made.

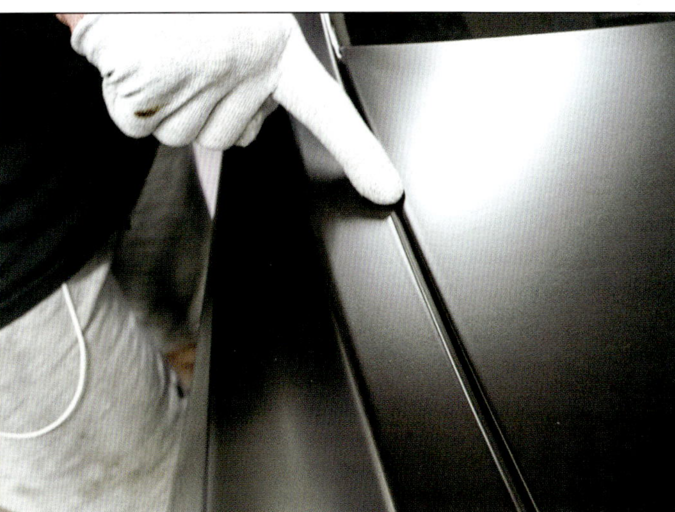

To ensure that all air has been released and no bubbles are trapped along the edge, wear a wrap glove and run your finger along the cut.

Work your way along the cut and follow the panel down toward the headlamp.

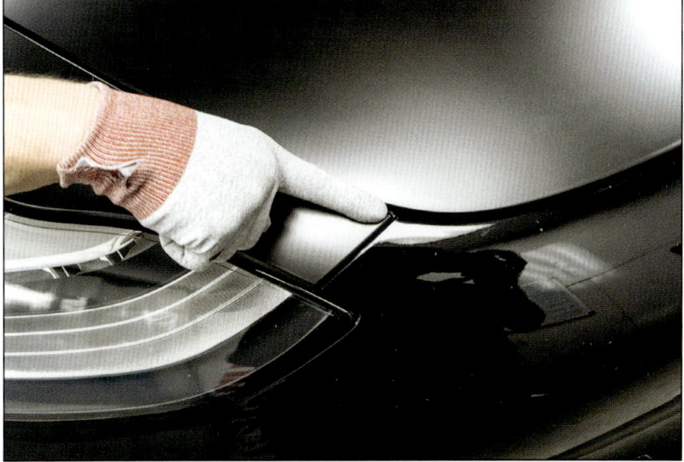

The installer is focused on getting the material to fold down into the gap between the hood and the fender, not completing a full tuck.

After completing all the cuts on a panel that you just installed, tuck the excess material in and wrap it around the edge of the panel. Doing this while wearing a wrap glove will make the process go much more smoothly.

Be cautious of creating trapped air before sealing off the panel and bunching up the loose material around the edges of the panel. Thankfully, there is an easy way to avoid both issues. Use your fingers to wrap the film around the edge of the panel. Always start before the edge of the panel and do not try to wrap the entire loose portion of the vinyl all at once. Focus on getting the edge of the vinyl securely down and allow the film to create a 90-degree angle throughout the entire edge. Repeat the step once again, only this time, the vinyl will make full contact with the underneath side of the panel.

There will be some areas of the vehicle where the manufacturer has placed weatherstripping along sec-

tions, such as those around the windows and between the windshield and the roof of the vehicle. Test these areas prior to wrapping the panel by checking the edge of the weatherstripping to see if it can be lifted. The majority of them can, and if so, never cut to the edge of the stripping and attempt to butt the material up against it or cut the film so that it lays over the top of the rubber.

Instead, cut the film so that you can lift the weatherstripping and

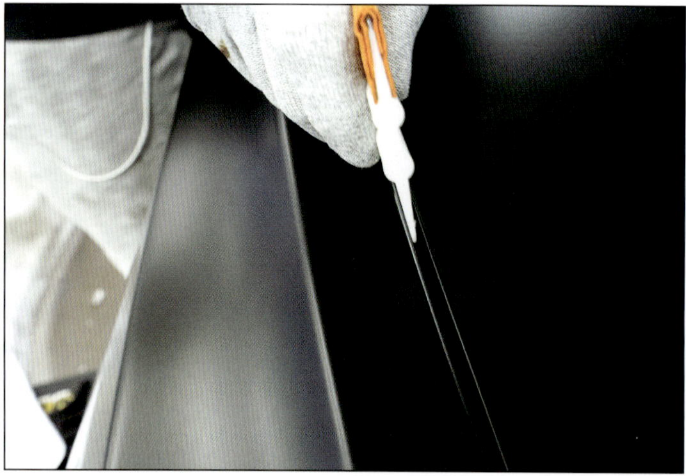

Run the hard edge of the squeegee at an angle toward the fender to establish a full tuck.

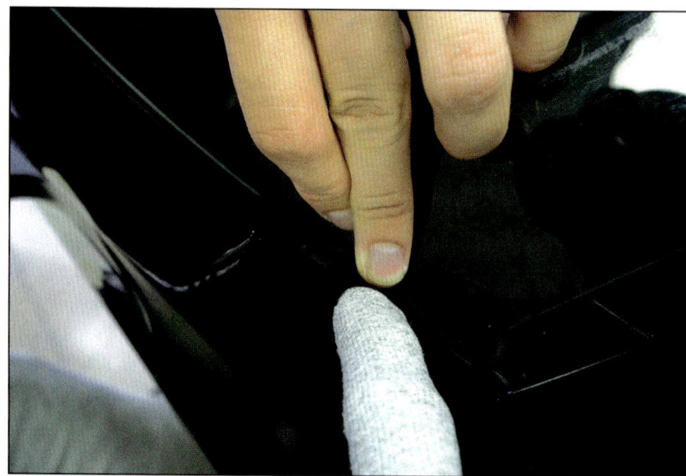

Always tuck the vinyl underneath any piece of weather-stripping that can be moved or lifted to allow access.

With the vinyl tucked underneath, the wrap has a cleaner, more professional look.

tuck the vinyl underneath. After you tuck in all the vinyl, the panel may look like it's complete, but there is one last important step to take care of: the "post heat."

Post Heating

Once the panel has been installed, it is common to want to move on to another section of the vehicle, but it is important not to do this.

Instead, post heat the panel immediately after its installation. Do this by applying heat to the panel with a heat gun. With the heat gun turned on, give it a few seconds to warm up and point it toward the panel.

Keep the nose of the gun approximately 4 to 5 inches away from the vehicle's surface. Move the tip of the gun in a slow, circular motion. Begin at one corner of the panel and move the gun in manner that slowly encompasses the entire area of the panel.

Pay close attention to how the vinyl reacts to the heat. One of the reasons for this process is to find out where the vinyl has not been fully pressed down and adhered to the surface. In an area where the vinyl has not been pressed down enough, the vinyl will rise from the surface and form a bubble. When this happens, either turn the gun off or point it away from the panel to give the area a chance to cool. This will only take a few seconds. Once it has cooled, press the area back down with your finger so that the vinyl is firmly adhered to the car. It is common to find a few small areas of the panel to react this way during the post-heating phase. After all, this is precisely one of the reasons for this process.

Once the issue has been addressed, heat the rest of the panel and stop each time you see any movement or bubble forming. Correct the area by letting it cool and pressing the material back down to the panel's surface. Pay close attention when heating any areas where the vinyl either is going into a recess or could be under high tension. Heating these areas will allow the film to relax and help prevent that area from failing.

When you immediately post heat the panel that was just installed, you lessen and possibly eliminate issues that the client might experience in the first few weeks after an install. Therefore, an experienced, professional installer will never skip this step.

The post-heating procedure is an important step and should be performed immediately after each panel is installed. Apply heat to the surface of the vinyl with a heat gun and hold the tip of the heat gun approximately 4 to 5 inches away from the panel. Move the heat gun in a small, circular motion as the entire panel is heated. Spend a few seconds on each section to allow the vinyl to reach post-heat temperature. Never stay in one spot for longer than 4 to 5 seconds to ensure that the material isn't overheated.

This is a pillar on a Tesla Model X shortly after the vinyl has been installed. Notice the bubble that has formed during a routine post heat. Bubbles such as these will appear when the vinyl has not been pressed down with enough pressure during install.

Bubbles are a common occurrence when it comes to wrapping vehicles, but they are easy to fix. Apply a low amount of heat, and while using a wrap glove, press down firmly and slowly at the center of the bubble until you feel the vinyl adhere to the car and lay down flat.

This is a wider shot of the pillar after the bubble was removed. Most quality vinyl comes with an air-release feature. This is a technology that places microscopic holes in the film during the manufacturing process that allow air to escape when pressing out bubbles. The Avery SW-900 series, the 3M 1080, and the 3M 2080 all have this feature. It is a good idea to purchase a material that has the air-release feature. Those that do not will be more difficult to install.

Resolving Issues

Here is an area of debris that was either trapped while the vinyl was being installed or not prepped properly. Because the vinyl is so thin, even the smallest bit of debris can be visible.

You will encounter issues during an installation, especially when the goal is to complete a full color change. Through years of installing vinyl-wrap material, I cannot recall a full color change where I did not find at least one or two items that needed correction.

The question isn't whether or not there will be an issue but rather what can be done as an installer to lessen the number of issues. A professional installer knows how to avoid unfortunate situations, and this ability usually comes from experience. In this chapter, we'll examine how to prevent and learn from common mistakes.

Steps to Avoid Problems

Most issues occur from contaminants that find their way to the underside of the vinyl and become trapped between the surface of the vehicle and the adhesive side of the film.

Keeping a clean environment will greatly reduce this from happening, but there are a few things that installers can do to help as well. Clean hands and clean clothes are required.

When you begin installing a new section of the vehicle and have just removed the backing from the film, never allow anyone to step in front of the adhesive side of the material.

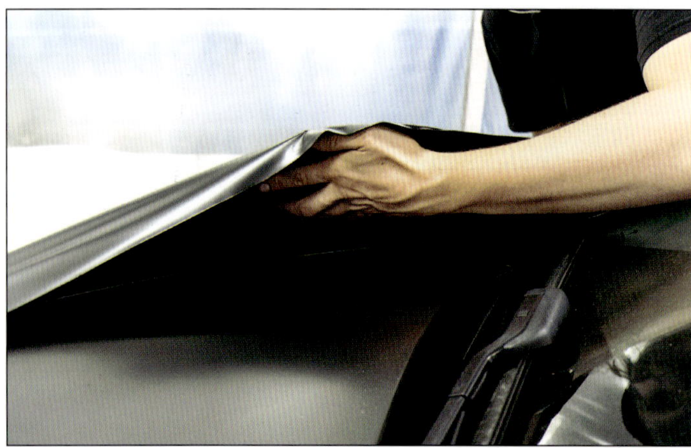

There are times when the material needs to be lifted to make adjustments during the install. Pay close attention when doing so, and never place your hands underneath the vinyl.

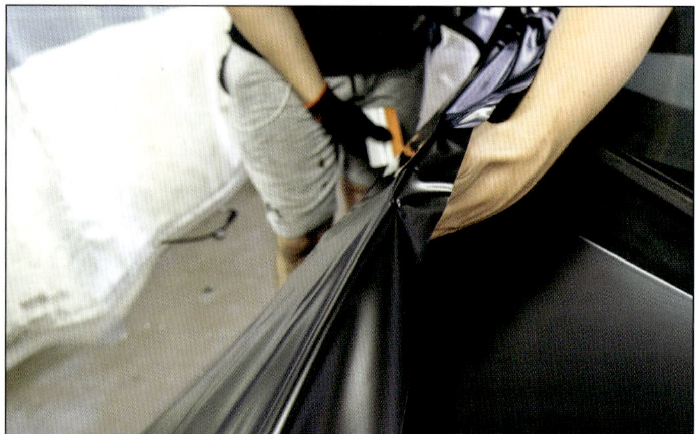

You may think your hands are clean, but even the tiniest speck of dust can be pulled off your hands and cause debris that becomes lodged between the panel and the vinyl.

Pull up a portion of the vinyl and pull it tight. When doing so, avoid placing your hands and arms underneath the vinyl.

The film often carries a static charge, and if someone steps in between the film and the vehicle, there is a good chance that static will pull tiny particles from the person's body and clothes onto the adhesive.

Pulling the Vinyl Up

There are various situations where you may be required to pull up a portion of the vinyl. When doing so, avoid placing your hands and arms underneath the vinyl. This is a last resort because in most cases you can easily pull the material off the car by heating the section and lifting the excess material from the edge that will eventually be cut and discarded.

It is important that the installer watches closely when applying the film. Most issues will either happen or make themselves visible during the squeegee phase of the install. It is imperative that you see it when it occurs. Do not ignore it; it will be much easier to handle before the cut-and-tuck phase than to try to fix it after the entire panel has been wrapped.

Using Heat to Solve Issues

A high-tension mark is an issue. It can either show itself as one or multiple lines in the film when the installer has failed to lift the material to feed it into a high recessed area and has forced the film into position with a squeegee or hand when the tension of the material was too high.

These tension lines are visible right away as the installer is laying the area. Immediately after you notice it, lightly heat the area and lift that portion of film from the car. This will release all tension. With the tension removed, slowly heat the area with the low setting of the gun until the lines fade away.

Re-lay the portion of vinyl, and this time do so with one portion of the vinyl lifted off the vehicle to refrain from placing the same amount of unwanted tension as was done previously.

Color Distortion

Color distortion occurs when the material has been heated and overstretched during installation. Depending on how far it has been stretched, there is still a chance that you will be able to restore its original color by using heat.

If the area has already been laid onto the vehicle, heat the area before pulling the material from the car. With no tension on the piece and with it pulled away from the car, hold the vinyl loosely with one hand and apply heat to the distorted section using the gun with your other hand. Watch the film as you are doing so. The material should shrink back to its original size. In doing so, the color will usually return as well.

Tears and Rips

Occasionally, a portion of the vinyl will break or tear during the installation of a panel. Unfortunately, it may lead to starting over with a new piece of film. This can cost time and money. Some materials are naturally more prone to rips and tears than others. For example, a film with a matte finish is much more brittle than one that is satin or gloss. However, there are some things you can do to keep from experiencing mishaps.

Room temperature is one of the most overlooked ways to make a mistake when it comes to rips and tears. The colder your environment, the easier it will be for the material to tear. This is especially true for films with a matte finish. It can be deceiving when an installer is used to wrapping in a normal room-temperature setting and switches to a colder environment. To correct this, avoid wrapping in a setting that is cooler than 75°F.

There will come a time when you have an imperfection, such as a wrinkle or color distortion, in an area of vinyl that has already been laid. These can be fixed but require the installer to peel a portion of the vinyl up from the vehicle to do so. This is another instance where the vinyl could tear. There are a few steps to take prior to lifting that minimize the risk.

First, use the heat gun and warm the entire surface of the area that needs to be lifted. Place your hand on the vinyl to ensure that this area is nice and warm. Once the material has been heated, pull the vinyl up slowly. If it is pulled too hard or too quickly, it could tear. If the vinyl cools down during this process, stop and apply another round of heat. In this instance, it is better to be safe than sorry. It is always better to pull warm vinyl that has been heated than it is to pull it cold.

Finally, when installing a panel, it is helpful to use a blade to cut away excess portions of vinyl as you go. Be careful when doing this. A straight cut through a portion of vinyl that is not needed may be dangerous if it is close to a portion you want to keep. It is much safer to make your cut rounded in areas like these, and it will reduce the risk of a potential tear.

Vehicle Disassembly

Many times, an installer will run into problems when attempting to wrap around obstacles on the car. Some items on a vehicle require more skill than others to remove, so each installer must determine whether they are capable of doing so.

However, many parts can be removed with little mechanic training. Emblems, washer nozzles, and moldings should never be ignored. Failure to remove parts can cause headaches when installing panels. Do not get in a hurry to install the vinyl and forget to remove these pieces because they have the potential to cause difficulties during the install.

Planning

Before you begin to wrap a panel, take a moment to stand back and visualize the panel being installed. Whether it is a fender, bumper, door, or trunk, each panel is shaped differently and requires a slightly different technique. It is better to have a game plan in mind and observe the shape

When film is laid down and stretched beyond its capabilities, it causes a stress in the film. This tension line is a visible imperfection, and although you need to look closely, it's not what you want in a beautiful vehicle wrap. Laying the film back down, unstressing it, and heating it up will cause the film to heal itself.

of the panel before you begin the installation.

If wrapping with a partner, bounce a few ideas off each other and discuss which approach you'll be using. You will become more familiar with this process with experience, and you will find out that a preplanned approach to a certain panel will reduce the number of issues you might encounter while installing the panel.

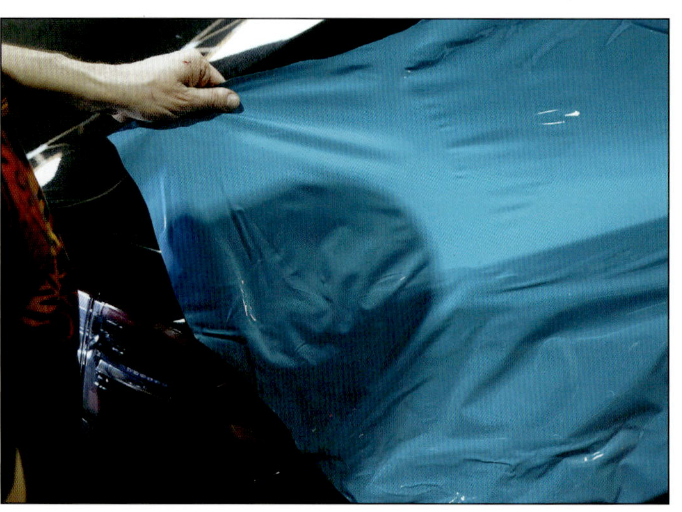

To fix the high-tension area, go back to where it started. Pull the vinyl back up until the place that the tension occurred or the visible tension line. It is important to go a bit past the high-tension line area and restart with a better approach.

Wrapping a Car Step by Step

One of the great things about wrapping a vehicle is that the list of basic tools to get started is fairly short and rather inexpensive. Many of these tools are explained in greater detail in Chapter 5.

Here is the list:

You have a new project and are ready to get started. You have the material, vehicle, and proper workspace and are ready to dig in. This chapter will direct you, step by step, how to make your new project a success.

We'll cover various installation techniques as they pertain to specific areas of the vehicle. However, first we'll discuss how to remove parts from the vehicle to speed up installation and ensure that the finished project is exactly as it was envisioned.

Vehicle Disassembly

Whether you do a full color change, partial wrap, or install a stripe kit, odds are good that there will be a few parts and pieces that need to be removed from the vehicle prior to installation. Installing vinyl wrap can be a lot like painting a vehicle when it comes to preparation, and a painted look is the goal.

With that being said, focus on accomplishing certain goals, such as minimizing the number of seams on the vehicle, obtaining full coverage on every panel, and staying away from wrapping around parts that may put a high amount of tension on the vinyl. There are several parts on a vehicle that are typically removed prior to each install. Here are a few of the most common.

Door Handles

To give a clean, professional, just-painted look, many vehicles

Vinyl Wrap Tools

- Wrap squeegee that comes with a hard plastic edge on one side and a felt edge on the other
- An Olfa or other comparable stainless-steel blade to cut the vinyl
- A heat gun, preferably one with an adjustable temperature dial, that plugs into a 110-volt outlet and comes with two different speeds
- Two squirt bottles. Fill one with diluted rubbing alcohol and the other with an all-purpose cleaner.
- One 16-foot measuring tape
- Two rolls of knifeless tape
- Microfiber cloths. Buy a pack of 36, as you will use them frequently.
- Vinyl film. The Avery SW-900 series, 3M 1080, or 3M 2080 is preferred.
- A set of plastic pry tools used to remove pieces from the vehicle
- Basic set of tools consisting of rachets, socket sets, pliers, etc.
- Infrared heating lamp. This one is more of a want than a need, as they can cost around $100, and you may be able to get by without. ■

require the door handles to be removed prior to installation. There are a few exceptions, such as the Nissan 370Z and the Ford Raptor, where the area that surrounds the handle can be wrapped up to the handle, but most handles are located in front of a door cup that you want to wrap without adding a second piece of vinyl to avoid a seam.

The good news is that most door handles use similar designs, and once you become familiar with how they operate, you will ultimately become more comfortable with the removal process. Once the handles have been removed, the side mirrors need to be addressed.

Side Mirrors

The decision to remove the side mirrors ultimately comes down to the design of the vehicle. Once again,

A vehicle that has a piece surrounding the door handle, such as this 370Z, can be wrapped without removing the handle prior to wrapping the door. Tape off the edge of the area, wrap the entire door panel, cut out the vinyl (allow for an extra inch of material to lift and tuck into the surrounding piece), and cut around the handle once it has been tucked in.

Most door handles look like these in some fashion. They are typically placed floating above a door cup and need to be removed to wrap the door panel without any seams.

A mirror located above the door trim gives the installer the option to remove it or not remove it prior to wrap installation. I often remove the mirror if I have already removed the door panel because most of the work has already been done.

In cases where the mirror is located under the window trim, remove the mirror from the door panel to wrap the panel without any seams.

In most cases, the inner door panel needs to be removed to access the bolts holding the mirror in place. Once the bolts have been loosened, disconnect any power connectors and remove mirror from the panel.

Once the mirror has been removed, the cleaning process can begin, and the vinyl can be installed without any obstructions.

the goal is to avoid adding a seam, so if the mirror is located under the window trim, it needs to be removed. A mirror located above the window trim will give the installer the option on whether to remove it. In this case, consider different factors, such as ease of removal and whether you plan to lay the entire side of the vehicle in one piece. Examine the vehicle and decide on a strategy beforehand to eliminate issues during the install.

A nicely wrapped mirror can pair well with a car featuring multiple colors. Here, the mirror adds extra black content to an A-pillar and tinted windows.

Front Bumper Inserts

There are times when it is a good idea to remove front bumper inserts prior to the install. Grille pieces and fog lights can be difficult to get the

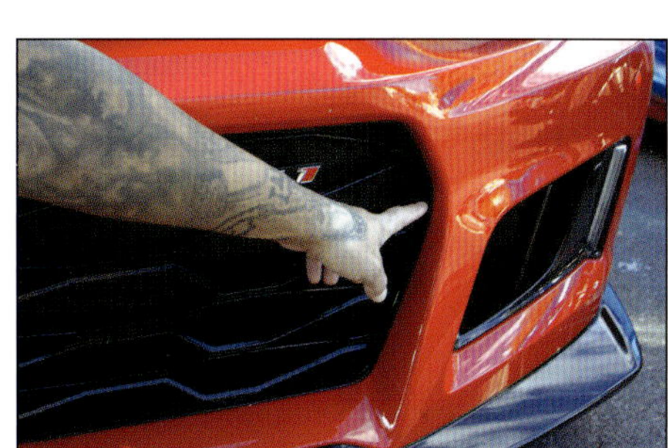

The bumper has been removed from the vehicle and placed onto a bumper stand to remove the plastic inserts. With the inserts removed, the bumper can be clipped back onto the front of the vehicle for the cleaning stage prior to wrap installation.

This curve located next to the grille puts a lot of tension on the vinyl if it is forced into this area. Instead, recognize where these high-tension spots will be before wrapping. Use the inlay method to cancel out the tension. Placing an inlay prior to laying the main front bumper piece will eliminate tension, reduce the chance of lifting, and provide a much less visible seam than if a piece was laid here afterward.

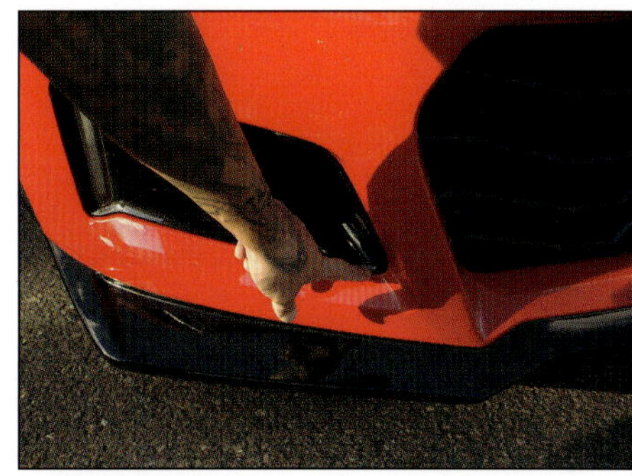

There are many places on a vehicle that force the vinyl into unwanted high-tension areas. The front bumper is where many of these areas exist. Observe panels like these and try to predict where the tension will occur before starting the installation process.

Here is another spot (located next the fog-light area) that holds a lot of tension. An experienced installer is able to recognize these areas and place inlays to combat the tension. The inlay is placed prior to the front bumper piece, and the edges of the inlay follow the natural body lines of the vehicle.

vinyl underneath. If you decide to wrap the bumper with them intact, be extremely cautious not to show any bleed from the original factory paint. In most cases, the bumper must be removed from the vehicle to get these pieces out, as most inserts clip in from the backside.

Antennas

When wrapping the roof of a vehicle, you may want to remove the antenna before wrapping the panel. Doing so will speed up the install, allow you to wrap the roof without having to wrap around the piece, offer a cleaner install, and guarantee no unwanted tension in that area. Antennas on most BMW models are simply a cap held on by adhesive. Most antennas from other companies require a

Inspect the area around the headlights when determining whether to remove them before wrapping the panel. Try inserting the tip of the blade between the panel and headlight casing. If there is room for the blade to be inserted, the headlights can remain. Simply tuck the vinyl around them when installing the panel.

small portion of the headliner located at the rear to be popped loose. The assembly holding the antenna in place is under the headliner.

Headlights and Taillights

Based on the original color of the vehicle and the color of the wrap, it may be wise to remove both headlights and taillights from the vehicle.

Taillights are typically easy to remove, and in many cases, they are worth the time to uninstall. On the other hand, headlights may require the removal of the front bumper. Ascertain whether there is enough space to tuck the vinyl in and around the headlight area before deciding to remove it. If the front bumper is being removed, uninstall inserts, such as grille pieces, and remove the headlights at the same time.

Removing the Taillights

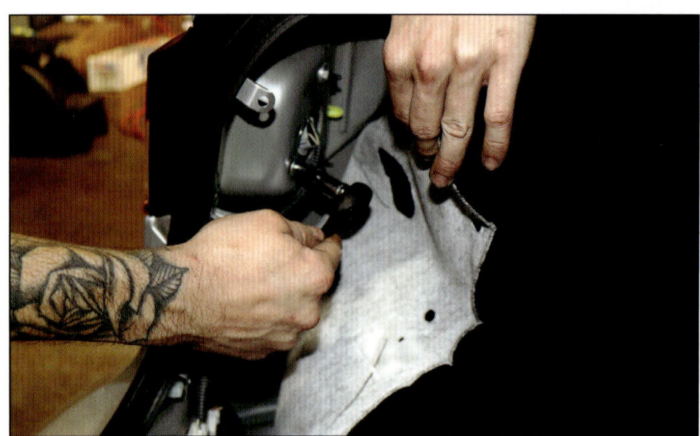

1 *Clips that attach the trunk liner may need to be removed. Many times, the bolts that keep the taillights in place are located behind the liner. Once the clips have been removed, pull back the liner and loosen the nuts.*

2 *After loosening the nuts from the bolts, gently pull the taillight away from its housing.*

3 *Disconnect the power connector.*

4 *The area where the taillight once sat will be extremely dirty. Clean all the dust and debris from area prior to laying the vinyl. Even though you will only be wrapping about an inch inside the space, the entire area must be cleaned.*

5 *When all the taillight lenses have been removed, place all the hardware in a resealable plastic bag and keep it in a safe place until the wrap is completed and the lenses are ready to be reinstalled.*

Rear Spoilers

Spoilers located on the trunk of a vehicle should almost always be removed. Attempting to wrap around a piece like this will usually result in high-tension areas that can lead to the vinyl lifting after being exposed to the sun.

Removing a rear spoiler is typically a simple task. They are usually held on by adhesive, bolts, or both. Uninstalling a bolted-on spoiler often requires removing the liner from inside the trunk to access the nuts. A spoiler that is attached with adhesive can be removed using a heat gun to apply a small amount of heat and carefully sliding a piece of coated fishing line through the area to separate the spoiler from the trunk.

Removing a Bolted-on Spoiler

1 *Open the trunk and locate the clips that hold the liner in place.*

2 *Using a panel-popper tool, place the mouth of the tool under the clip and apply pressure to extract the face of the clip. Once it has been loosened, pull the clip out.*

3 *Continue following around the edge of the liner and remove the remainder of the clips.*

4 *Keep all of the clips in a resealable plastic bag to make sure that they do not get misplaced.*

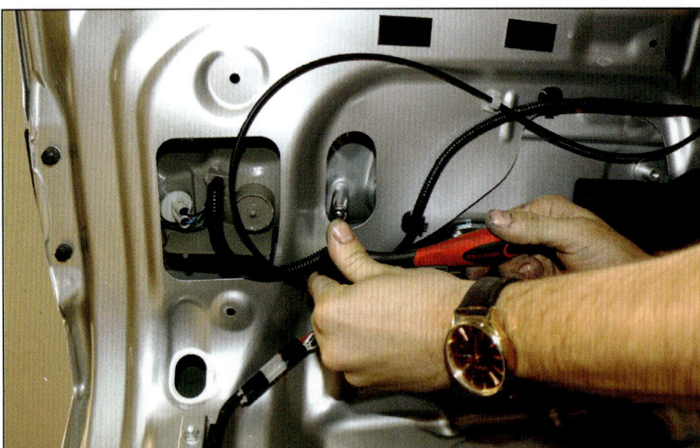

5 *When all the clips have been removed, remove the liner. Pay attention to any pieces that may be included in the liner. Typically, there is a safety trunk release latch that may require disassembly prior to removing the liner.*

6 *With the liner removed, use a flashlight to locate the bolts that hold the rear spoiler to the trunk.*

Removing a Glued-on Spoiler

1 *With the temperature dial just under maximum heat, use the heat gun and begin heating one edge of the spoiler. The object is to loosen the adhesive underneath the spoiler.*

2 *Slowly wave the gun back and forth about 3 to 4 inches away from the spoiler and work toward the middle of the piece.*

3 *Don't forget to heat the underneath portion of the spoiler and the top. There is no reason to heat the entire length of the spoiler. Just focus on heating up to its middle portion.*

4 *After the first half of the spoiler has been heated, feed a long piece of fishing line below the corner of the piece.*

5 *While firmly holding both ends of the fishing line, work to the center of the spoiler. Once you reach the middle, remove the fishing line, heat the other end of the spoiler, and repeat the process until you make your way through all of the adhesive at both ends.*

6 *Once all of the adhesive has been separated, place a firm hold on the spoiler and pull it from the trunk.*

7 *With the rear spoiler removed, place it in a safe area where it cannot be damaged. Now, focus on removing the remaining adhesive off the trunk that has been left behind by the piece.*

Wiper Nozzles

When installing a hood wrap, remove the wiper nozzles that are located directly on the surface of the panel. Open the hood and remove the plastic clips that hold the liner underneath. Detach the hoses from each nozzle. Squeeze the clips that hold the nozzle in place with a pick tool and push upward to remove the nozzle from the panel.

Wiper Nozzle Removal

1 Clean the hood area to prepare for installation. Both the Jeep emblem and the windshield wiper pumps need to be removed before the prep stage can begin. How to remove emblems is discussed on the next page, so we will go over how to remove the wiper pumps. These are easy to remove and will make the hood installation quicker and easier to complete.

1a Begin by opening the hood and finding the tube that supplies the cleaning solution to the pumps. If you do not see it right away, it may be hidden underneath the hood liner. Remove the clips that hold the liner in place and take out the liner if necessary.

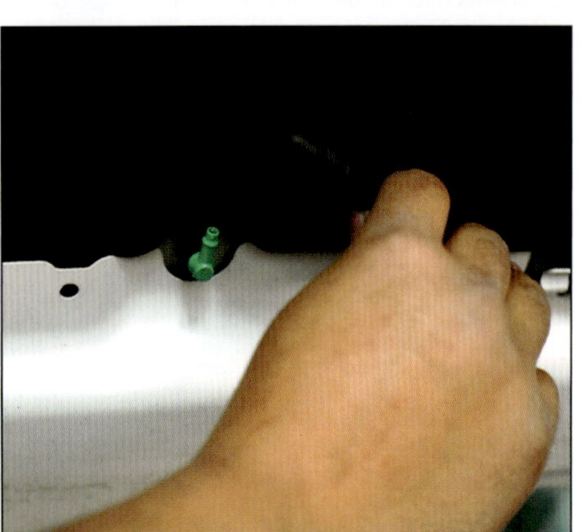

2 Follow the tube that supplies the liquid to the nozzles and disconnect it from the nozzle.

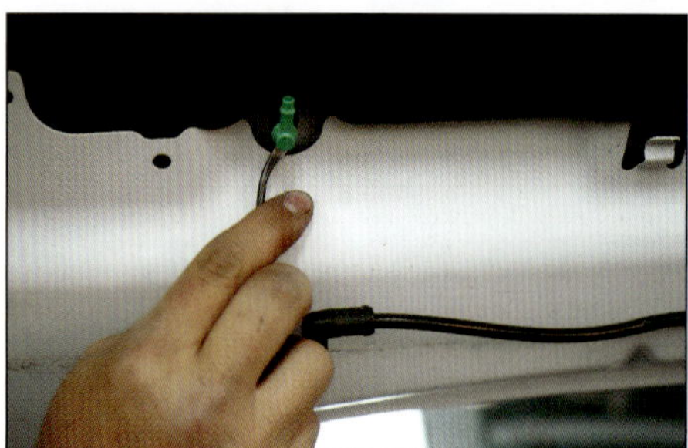

3 There are two tabs that hold the nozzles in place. The tabs are located on either side of the nozzle or at the top and bottom of the nozzle (as shown here). Depress each tab with a pry tool to release the nozzle.

4 Remove the nozzle by pulling it out from the top of the hood. This entire process only takes a few minutes. The hood panel can now be wrapped without any obstacles.

Badges/Emblems

Never attempt to wrap around badges or emblems. These pieces are typically held on by adhesive. Heat the area with a heat gun and run coated fishing line carefully under the piece to remove it from the vehicle.

Use an adhesive remover that will not harm clear coat to remove any adhesive left behind. A few emblems, such as those located on the hood and front grille, may be attached with pins and/or nuts. Observe the back portion of these emblems prior to removal and remove any necessary attachments.

Keep all emblems in the glove box of the vehicle you are wrapping. There is nothing more frustrating than completing an amazing wrap and having a missing emblem during the reassembly phase.

Preparation and Removal of Emblems and Badges

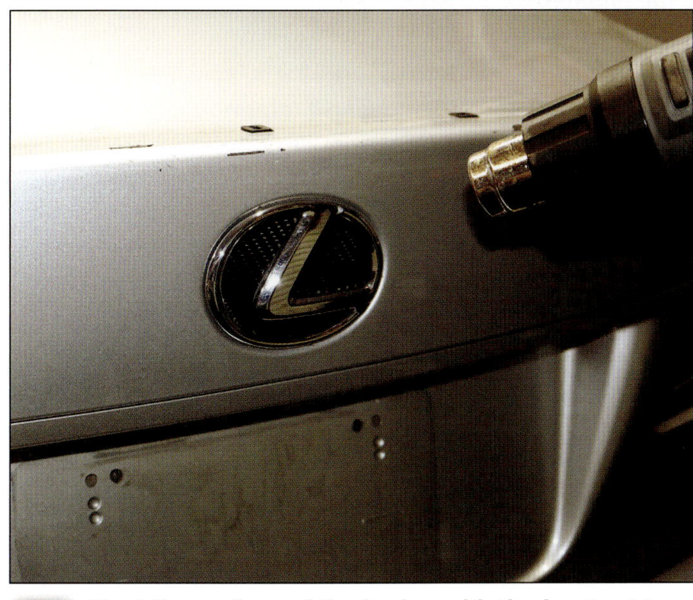

1 *Heat the surface of the badge with the heat set to high and the tip of the gun 3 to 4 inches away from the emblem.*

2 *Slowly wave the heat gun back and forth until the entire surface of the badge has been heated.*

3 *Immediately after heating the badge, slide a piece of coated fishing line under the edge of the emblem.*

4 *Use a firm grip and a back-and-forth sawing motion to work the fishing line through the adhesive beneath the emblem.*

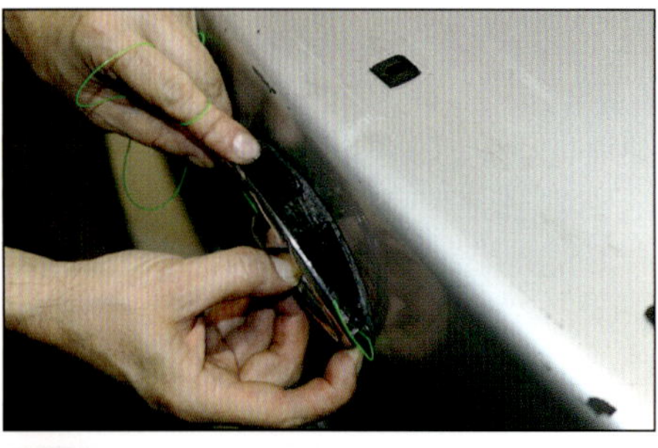

5 *Once the fishing line is through the adhesive, grip the badge and pull firmly to remove it.*

6 *There may be small pins located behind the emblem that were used by the factory to align the badge on the vehicle. In these cases, the fishing line may need to be repositioned to work around the pins.*

7 *Finish removing the emblem from the vehicle.*

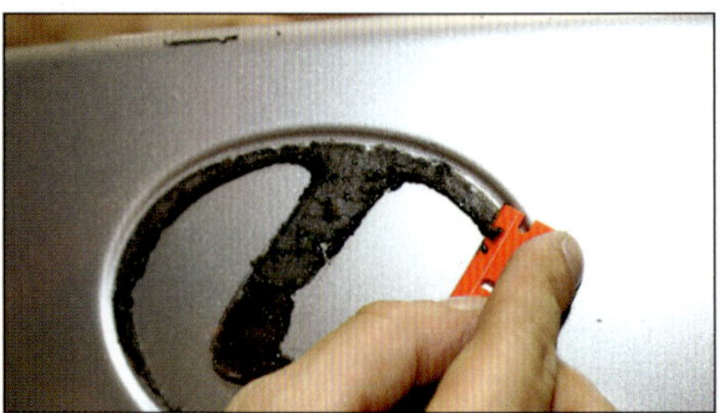

8 *Now that the emblem has been removed, the next step is to remove the adhesive.*

9 *Spray a liberal amount of adhesive remover on the residue and let it set for a few minutes.*

10 *After the remover has set on the old adhesive, use a plastic razor blade to slip beneath the adhesive to remove it. These blades are inexpensive and typically can be purchased in a large pack that will last numerous installs.*

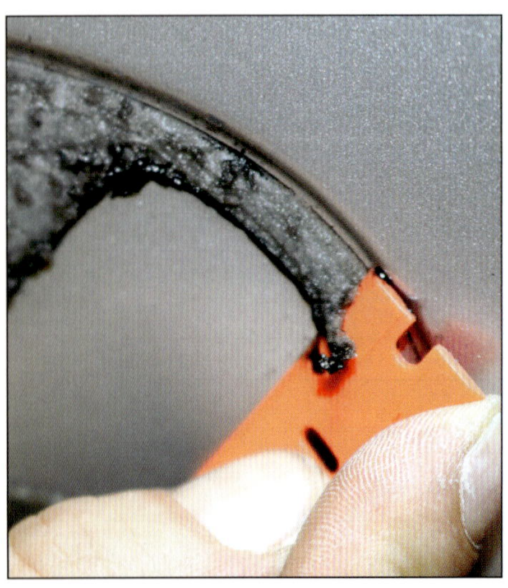

11 *The plastic razor blade provides the nice sharp edge needed to remove the adhesive without scratching the paint.*

12 *It will take some time and patience; every bit of adhesive must be removed from the area. This requires working through the many layers and spraying adhesive remover several times while allowing time to soak between layers.*

13 *Do not forgot to place loose emblems inside a resealable plastic bag so that they will be easy to find later.*

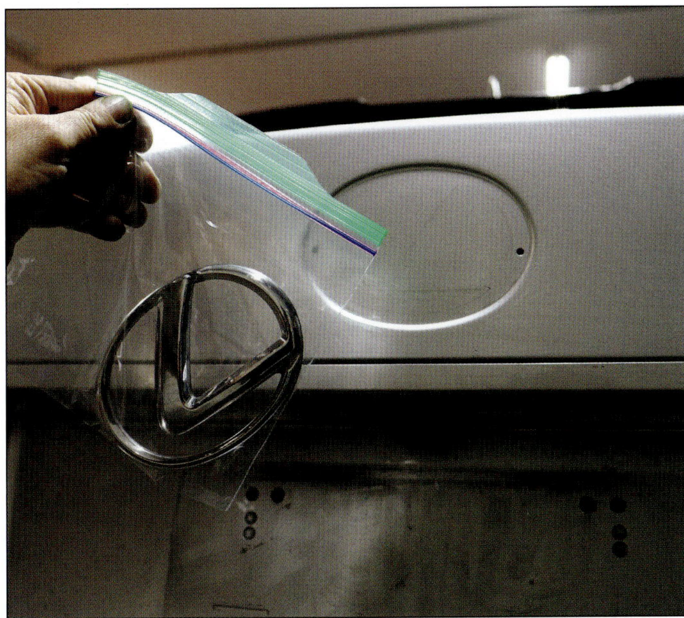

14 Notice that all of the adhesive has been removed from where the badge once was.

15 Keep all emblems in the glove box of the vehicle that is being wrapped. There is nothing more frustrating than being unable to find an emblem during the reassembly phase after completing an amazing wrap.

Cleaning and Preparation

We cannot overstate how important it is to have a clean surface prior to your install. Most of the color-change vinyl used will typically be around 3 mil in thickness. Because the vinyl is characteristically thin, any type of debris that might be stuck to the surface will ultimately show through the vinyl. A small speck of dust or a human hair stuck between the surface of the vehicle and the vinyl can be so much of an eyesore that the installer will remove the vinyl and start again with a new piece of material.

Therefore, do not skip steps during the cleaning process. Time spent on cleaning will give the project a professional look and will potentially save time and money in the long run. To achieve an acceptable level of cleanliness, the following process is recommended.

If you get a hair, piece of dirt, or any other contaminant underneath the wrap, heat the area and pull the film up slowly to expose the dirty area. There are instances when you are able to use the tip of a blade to clear the area of the debris.

If a contaminant gets underneath the wrap, heat the area and pull up the film slowly. Sometimes, the debris can be cleared by using the tip of your blade.

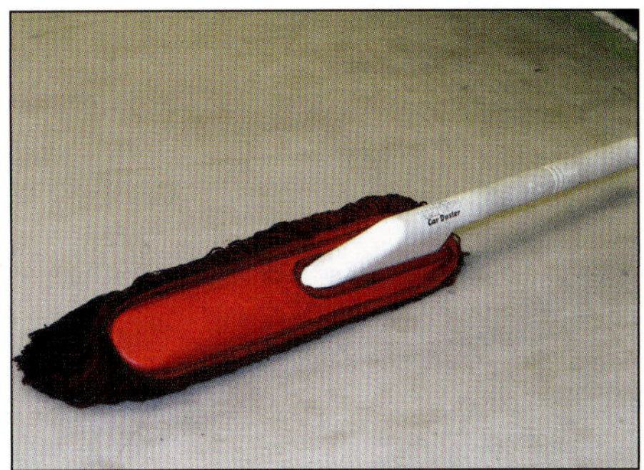

The California Duster can be purchased at most auto supply chains for about $15. These dusters work well to remove the top layer of dust off any wrapped panel. Best of all, they will not scratch the vinyl while doing so.

Shop around and find a nice thick, high-quality microfiber cloth to use in your shop. These cloths will be used during the cleaning process. Always use a separate cloth for each stage of cleaning. These cloths are also ideal for cleaning a full wrap after the vinyl has been installed.

When preparing to wrap a vehicle, don't forget any inconspicuous areas that may hide dirt and grime. The areas underneath the wheel wells can be easily over-looked and often contain a level of debris that works against the vinyl's adhesive and results in unwanted lifting.

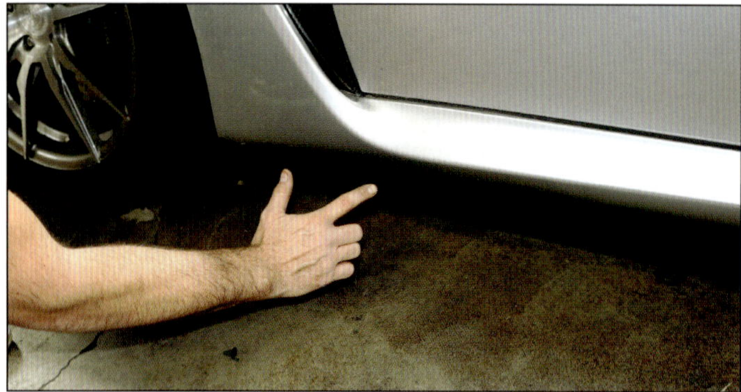

The area at the bottom of the rocker panels is notorious for being filthy. Pay close attention when it comes to cleaning these areas, and do not forget to clean underneath. Heavy grime, such as road tar, won't be removed easily with an all-purpose cleaner. It may require an adhesive remover to ensure that this area is fully clean. Inspect the area thoroughly before continuing to the alcohol phase of cleaning.

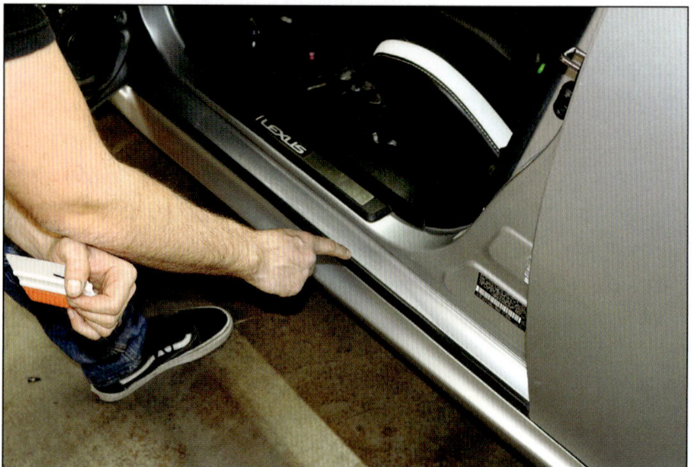

When wrapping the area below the door, feed the wrap onto the doorjamb after the vinyl has been cut. Be careful because these areas are often dirty. Open the door and clean this area well before beginning the installation.

This is an area that is often forgotten during the cleaning phase. The material used to wrap the door panel needs to adhere firmly to this small section behind the door. If this area is not cleaned properly, the vinyl will fail and may require the entire door panel to be reinstalled.

First, carefully remove any loose dust or debris using a California duster or microfiber cloth. If you have access to a water source, a quick power wash to accomplish this task is beneficial.

Second, go over each panel of the vehicle with an all-purpose cleaner and a microfiber cloth. This is going to be the most extensive stage of the cleaning process. Remove all areas of stubborn grime, grease, or tar.

Another area that is often left out during the cleaning phase is the small edge underneath the hood. Take the time to open the hood and clean this area thoroughly before attempting to install the hood panel.

Make sure that you open the trunk and clean the underneath edge of the trunk to remove all dirt and debris before you wrap this panel.

Wheel Wells

Parts of the vehicle that need extra attention will be located near the tires, under the wheel wells, and the lower portions of panels that are close to the road. During this stage, do not forget to open all doors, trunks, and hoods to properly clean inside the doorjamb areas and backside edges of these panels.

A piece of vinyl that has been separated from its backing will often hold a static charge. Because of this, areas that are holding trapped dust can easily spill debris onto the adhesive side of the vinyl during the install. To avoid this, pay close attention when cleaning nooks and crannies where dust may hide and collect, such as in between trim pieces and sections that are not getting wrapped (windows and side mirrors).

Now that you have cleaned with an all-purpose cleaner, take a moment to graze over the panel with the back of your hand. The surface should be smooth and free of any contaminants. If this is not the case, take time to clay bar the panel before moving to the next step.

The final step involves using a 70-percent isopropyl alcohol solution and microfiber cloth to wipe the entire panel. This will clear the surface of any remnants from the cleaning solution. The material for your panel should be cut and ready for install prior to this step as the installer should begin to lay the panel immediately after the final stage of cleaning has been completed.

Clay Barring the Car

1   *Applying a clay bar to the clear coat of a vehicle's paint is an effective way to ensure that all debris has been removed prior to installation.*

2 *Before using the clay bar on the vehicle, apply a light mist of water or cleaning solution to the surface.*

3 *With the clay bar in the palm of your hand, use long linear strides and go over the same area a few times until the surface of the clear coat turns smooth. Give the surface a few minutes for the clay to set and turn cloudy.*

4 *The next step is to remove the clay. Using an all-purpose cleaner, spray the panel and dampen a microfiber cloth with cleaner.*

5 *Use the microfiber cloth with a firm circular motion to remove the clay.*

Measuring and Cutting

Most vehicles require a roll of 25 yards of material to complete a full color change. This is typically enough vinyl to wrap the entire vehicle and have 3 or 4 yards extra if a few panels need to be rewrapped. Many color-change films have a width of 60 inches from left to right. This number is important to keep in mind when measuring panels.

For example, any panel that measures more than 60 inches in both directions needs to be seamed. Fortunately, on newer vehicles, not many need to be seamed. Another reason to keep that magic 60-inch number in mind is to help save material. Measure every panel of the vehicle first, write down all the measurements, and figure out if you

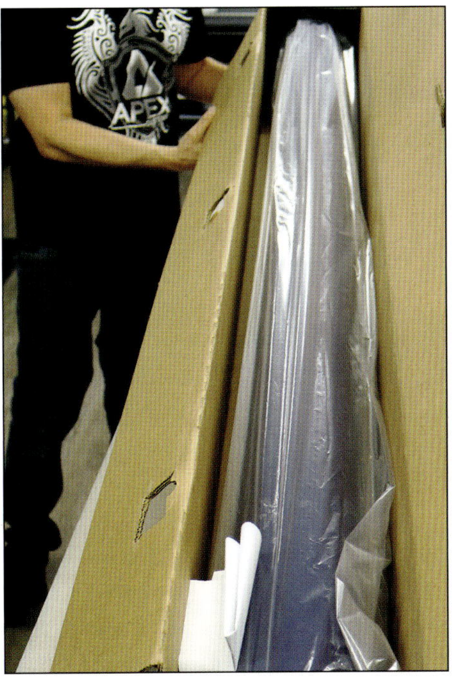

A full roll of color-change film will typically be 25 yards in length, which is 75 feet.

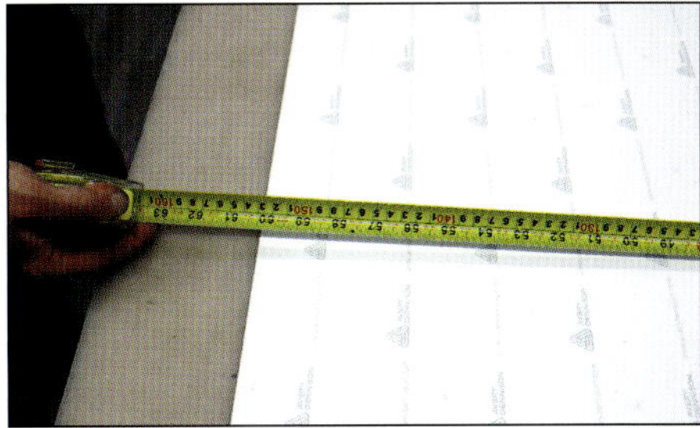

Although some chrome-colored films come in a 48-inch width, 60 inches is standard for most films used for full color changes.

can combine two panels into one 60-inch piece.

Saving material is important, but do not obsess about it to the point that it sacrifices quality. When possible, stay at least 4 to 5 inches (rather than 1 or 2) over the size of the panel in both directions.

Driver's Side and Passenger's Side Installation

There are two main techniques to consider when installing vinyl to both the driver's side and passenger's side of the vehicle. Each one is based on the number of panels that the installer will lay at one time.

Oftentimes, the rear quarter panel of the vehicle will be connected to an arm that runs above the windows and ends just before the fender. Because this section needs to be covered with one continuous piece, incorporate the door panels during the same installation. This method will save on material and speed up the installation.

Almost all vinyl wrap films will have a standard width of 60 inches. This is good to remember when measuring the panels, as you can easily round up to 60 if one direction of the panel measures in the 50s.

Once unpacked, remove the plastic sheath and the two plastic supportive pieces located on each end.

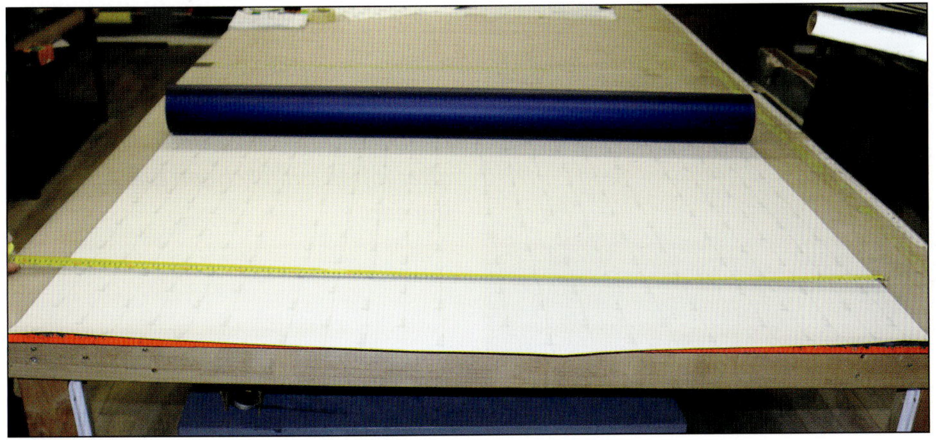

This rear quarter panel is connected to the A-pillar that ends just above the fender. In this case, it is better to wrap the rear quarter, A-pillar, and door panel with one big piece of vinyl.

The installer may also decide to include the fender panel and lay the entire side of the vehicle at once using one large piece with this method. When using a vinyl that offers color-shifting properties, this method is the best way to ensure consistency, and it guarantees that the vinyl will shift flawlessly.

The other approach when wrapping the driver's side or passenger's side is to wrap each panel individually. This method usually requires more time and material, but there are a few instances when this is recommended.

If your color change is drastic (the original paint is substantially different than the color of vinyl you are using), wrapping each side panel individually will allow for greater coverage and allow you to go further between the panels to ensure that the original color is hidden. This method is ideal for a solo installer, whereas laying multiple panels at once will require two or three installers to work in tandem.

Wrapping the Side

1 *When it comes to wrapping the side of a vehicle, an experienced vinyl wrap installer may consider wrapping multiple panels at once and installing the entire side of the vehicle with one long piece. This method can make the installation process move faster. This Camaro has been prepped and cleaned just prior to installation.*

2 *Two to three people are needed to place the vinyl onto the vehicle: one person at each end of the material and a third to peel the backing. This is how the vinyl will look after it has initially been placed onto the car.*

3 *Apply heat and tension to the vinyl to remove wrinkles and create a smooth surface. This will prepare the vinyl for the next step of the installation: applying pressure with the squeegee.*

4 *Treat the entire side of the vehicle as if it were one large panel. Begin applying pressure with the squeegee. Start at the top of the piece and work your way down. Don't advance too far in one section. Keep the same line of progression throughout the entire piece on all the panels. Once the entire side of the vehicle has been installed, it will look like this Camaro, which is ready to move on to the cutting phase.*

Wrapping a Quarter Panel

This is the driver-side fender from a 2019 Tesla Model 3. The camera located at the rear of the panel has been removed. The fender has been prepped and cleaned and is ready for installation. The following photos will go through each step as a single installer completes the panel.

1 *Use masking tape to get the vinyl in the proper position and place two magnets at one end to keep the vinyl in place. These magnets can be found online. They are relatively inexpensive and provide an extra hand when completing an installation by yourself.*

2 Bend the piece of vinyl back to where the magnets are placed.

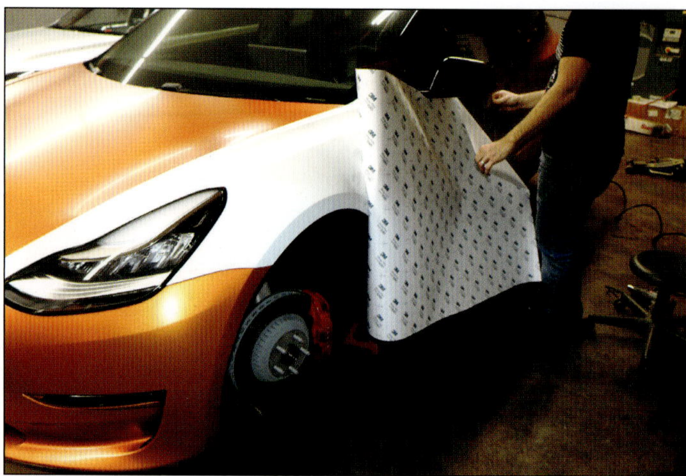

3 Remove the backing. Begin at the top corner of the vinyl and peel downward to expose the first foot or two of the vinyl.

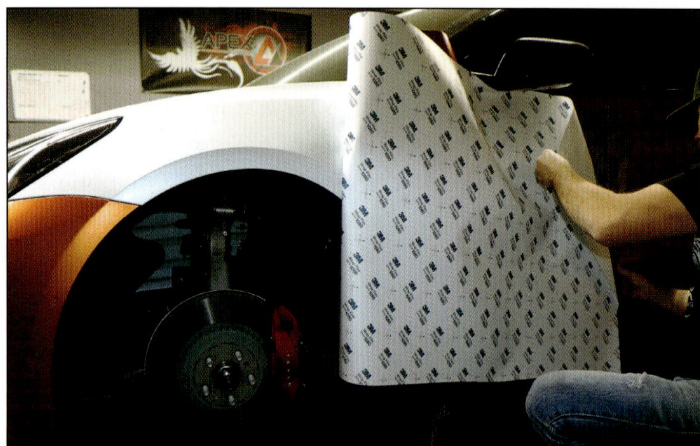

4 Using the exposed portion of the vinyl, double back the corner and adhere it to the vehicle as an anchor to hold the vinyl in place. Make sure that the area is clean, and keep in mind that this portion of the vinyl will exceed the far end of the fender and eventually be cut off and discarded as excess.

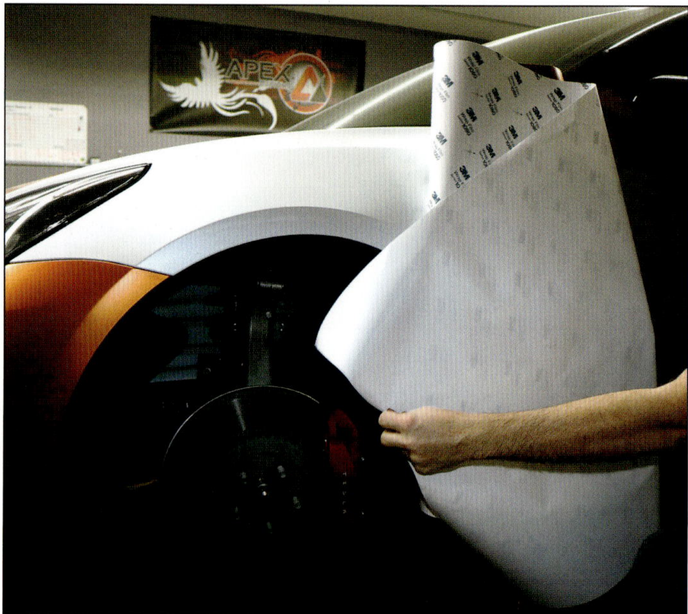

5 Now that the film has a firm anchor, continue pulling the backing away from the vinyl.

6 Avoid pulling from the middle section of the backing. Place a firm grip on the upper and lower edges of the backing and pull slowly in a continuous motion.

7 As the backing is pulled away, it can get in the way as it becomes larger. It is okay to pause for a second to remove the backing.

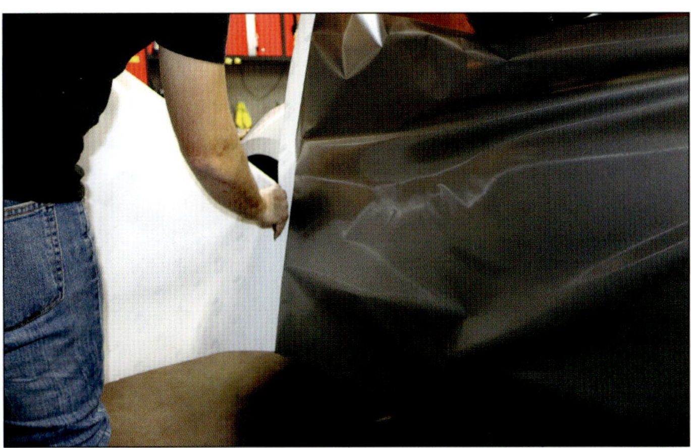

8 Cut through the backing and let it drop to the floor to continue the installation without being hindered. Continue removing the rest of the backing until the vinyl is fully exposed.

9 Now that the backing has been completely removed, with the vinyl away from the vehicle, heat the material with a heat gun. The tip of the gun should be a few inches away from the surface of the vinyl.

10 After the vinyl has been heated, it will become softer and easier to stretch. Pull it toward the front of the vehicle and wrap it around the top of the fender.

11 Once all of the backing has been removed, manipulate the film until it is stretched tight to the panel and has a smooth, wrinkle-free surface. Here, the installer makes a relief cut, starting at the headlamp area and ending a few inches short of the where the panel is. This will relieve some tension from the film and allow the vinyl to lay down smoothly without much effort.

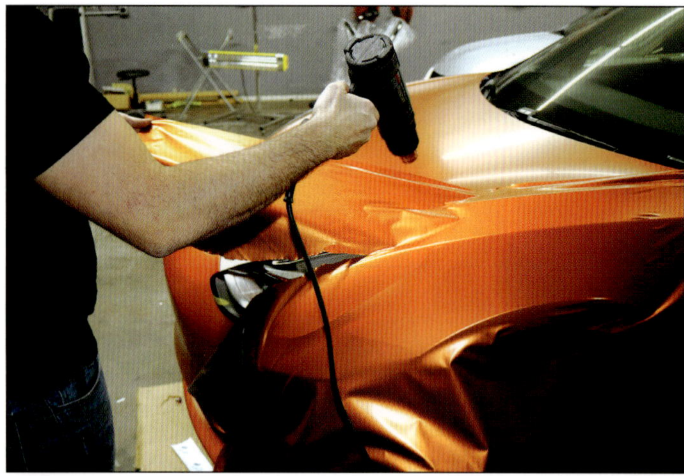

12 *After the relief cut has been made, slowly lift a portion of the vinyl away from the car. While holding the lifted portion of the film, apply low heat with a heat gun until the vinyl becomes warm and flexible.*

13 *After heating the film, give the material a slight pull to get a smooth appearance. However, never pull material that is too hot because it may distort the color. To avoid this, count to three and then start the pull.*

14 *The object here is to pull the material toward yourself as it is laid down. Manipulate it before it makes contact to the vehicle. Pull outward so that it lays down smooth. We call this process "reading the vinyl," which is basically learning and knowing which direction in which to pull the vinyl to lay it down with few to no wrinkles. It is easy to catch on to this process after you have done a few projects. Once you become familiar with reading the vinyl, the installs will take less time to complete.*

15 *Now that most of the wrinkles have been taken care of at the front half of the fender, we will focus on getting the rear of the panel laid down smoothly as well.*

16 *Grab the lower corner of the film, lightly pull the material away from the vehicle, and begin applying heat. The material will become softer and much more flexible. During the heating process, don't pull the film. Instead, hold the film loosely to avoid putting any unpleasant tension lines into the vinyl.*

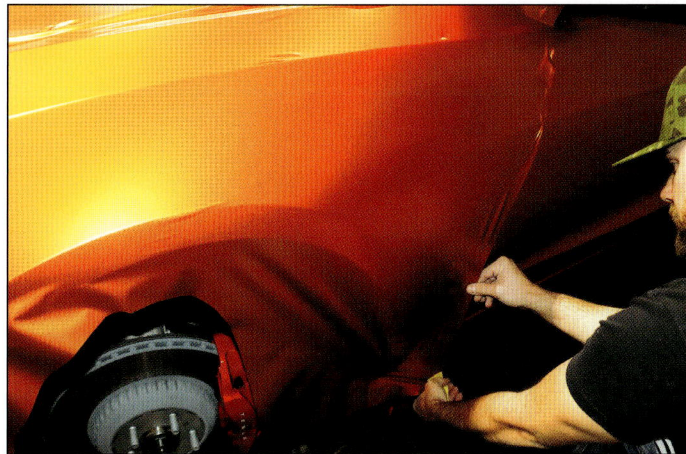

17 *As soon as you stop heating the vinyl, wait a few seconds to make sure the film is not too hot, and pull down on the vinyl. As you pull down, read the vinyl by pulling in the direction needed to remove the wrinkles just prior to the film contacting the vehicle.*

18 *Once the entire panel has been laid, there should be a consistently smooth surface that is virtually wrinkle free. Some installers like to cut away large portions of excess material before continuing to the next step and beginning to apply pressure with the squeegee.*

19 *While wrapping the quarter panel, pull the vinyl tight from the bottom to ensure an even application throughout the panel.*

Hood Application

Although every panel should be laid with care, the hood is often the main focal point of the wrap. When done correctly, it can really set off a great color change. Remember to remove wiper nozzles and any plastic inserts that may get in the way.

An assistant is highly recommended for the initial lay to help line up the panel and keep the material clean. A typical hood piece will usually measure in at around 75x60 inches, so it is important to focus on keeping the material from getting contaminated with any foreign debris. When the backing is removed, each installer needs to concentrate on keeping the piece as far up from the floor as possible. Stay a good distance away from the front end of the vehicle, as it is common for the vinyl to attract dust from the many trapped areas, such as the grille.

With one person on the driver's side and the other on the passenger's side, increase the amount of tension on the vinyl just before it touches the car. The vinyl should be wrinkle-free before applying pressure with the squeegee.

Choose a section in the middle area of the hood and work to one side while holding the squeegee at a 45-degree angle. Once one side has been completed, move back to the center of the panel and work out the other side.

Do not begin to make any cuts until the entire panel has been laid. If you see the vinyl begin to wrinkle during the install, lift the vinyl from the outer edge and apply heat until the surface becomes smooth again. Place the material back down onto the vehicle and continue applying pressure until the panel is complete.

Wrapping the Hood

1 *The hood panel is prepped and clean and ready for installation.*

2 *Hood panels are typically large, so a two-person installation is highly recommended.*

3 *The two installers hold the vinyl with the backing still attached in front of the hood panel.*

4 *The first installer peels the corner of the backing from the film and hands the corner to the second installer.*

5 *Remember to hold the vinyl off of the floor to prevent any dust or debris from contaminating the adhesive. Finish removing the entire piece of backing.*

6 *Both installers reposition their grip to prepare for the initial lay.*

7 *Both installers approach the vehicle with vinyl in hand.*

8 *Stretch the vinyl horizontally as initial contact is made with the vehicle.*

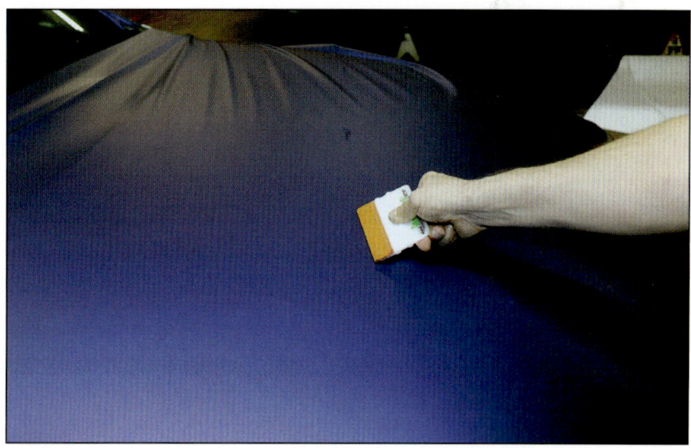

9 *Begin installing by applying pressure with the squeegee. Start in the middle of the panel and work out to one side.*

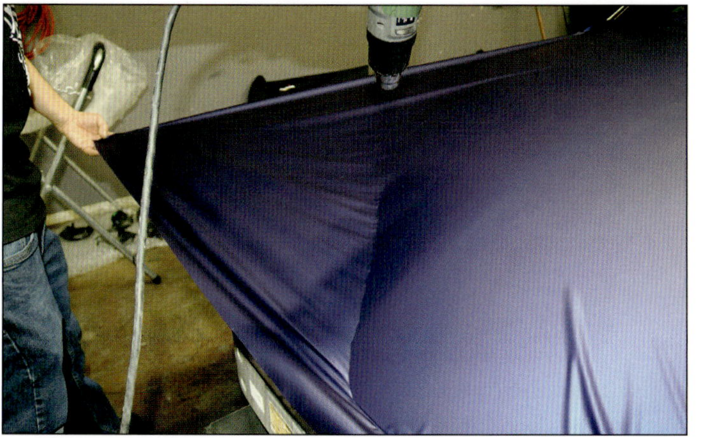

10 *As you get closer to the edge of the panel, the vinyl will begin to show wrinkles and need to be lifted to smooth out this section.*

11 With the vinyl lifted, apply heat to the top of the wrinkles.

12 As the temperature of the film rises, the wrinkles become more prominent. This is normal. Keep heating until they become smaller.

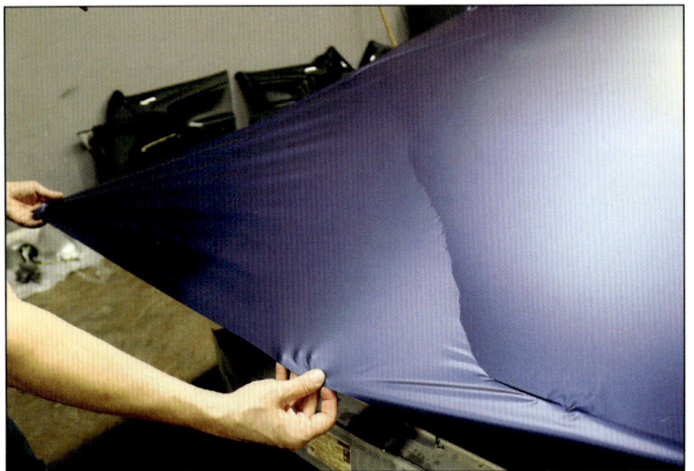

13 This is how the film looks after the wrinkles have been successfully heated out.

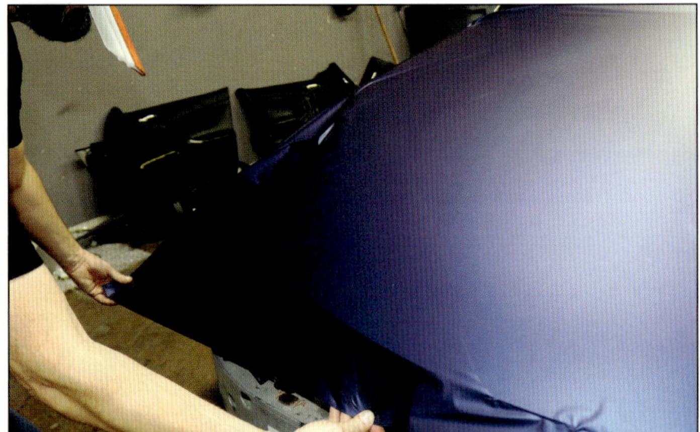

14 Now that the film has a nice smooth appearance, give it a slight stretch and lay it back down to the vehicle.

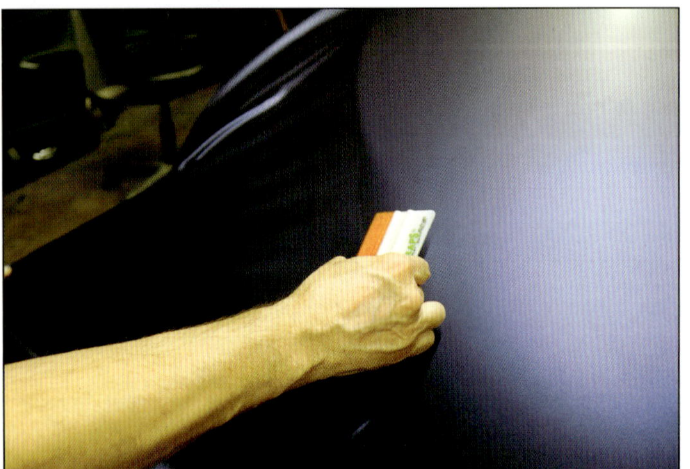

15 With the vinyl smooth and the wrinkles gone, resume applying pressure with the squeegee and continue working out toward the edge of the panel.

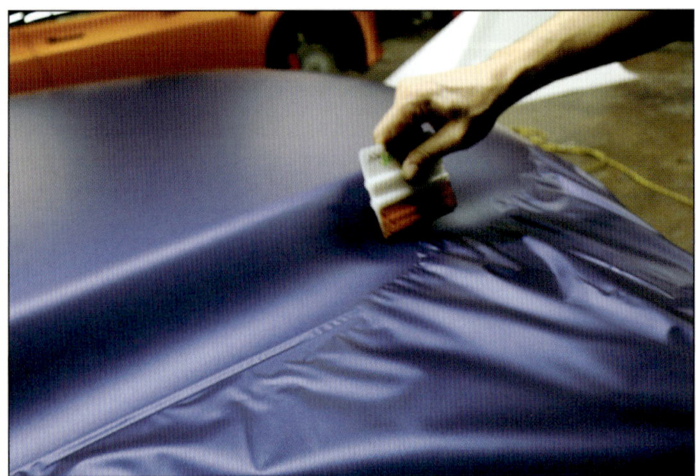

16 Once the material is bridged over to the fender, move on to the other side of the hood and repeat the steps to complete the panel.

Bumper Application

The front and rear bumper panels are two of the most difficult areas of any vehicle to wrap. Here are a few helpful methods to make these sections a little easier to master.

First, remove all plastic inserts, lights, etc. that may cause any obstructions. The front bumper receives the brunt of road debris, so pay close attention and clean this area meticulously. A bumper will have many curves and bends to it, and because of this, it is prone to fail after time out on the road.

Examine the bumper prior to installation to predict where the high-tension areas will be. To combat these tension areas, place inlays in inconspicuous areas before installing the full-size piece of vinyl onto the bumper. An inlay is a small piece of vinyl that goes down on the car first and allows the installer to relieve tension by making a relief cut in that area and leave the inlay located behind the main piece.

Inlaying the Front Bumper

1 *Most front bumpers require some inlays before the main piece can be installed. This is the first step on this Tesla Model 3 front bumper.*

2 *When done correctly, the inlays will relieve tension and increase the longevity of the wrap.*

3 *Focus on following the natural body lines of the car when determining the placement of the inlay.*

4 *Notice how the inlay flows with the body lines of the vehicle. All the cuts are straight and clean.*

Using an infrared heat lamp to install the front bumper makes it a much easier task.

For best-looking results, have the inlays follow the natural body lines of the car and use knifeless tape to ensure that all the edges are clean because these lines will be visible through the top piece of vinyl. After all the inlays have been placed and the bumper is clean, install the large piece of vinyl to complete the panel.

A typical bumper averages around 130 inches in length and 30 inches in height. Based on its large size, a two-person installation is highly recommended. The material must be heated as it is installed, so place heat guns within reach before removing the backing.

Although a heat gun is sufficient when wrapping a bumper, a self-standing infrared heating lamp offers a constant hands-free heat source to the vinyl that makes the initial lay go down with much less difficulty.

To begin the installation, have one person stand with one edge of the vinyl at the driver's side of the bumper and the other installer on the passenger's side. Remove the backing and be careful to not allow any debris to adhere to the adhesive side of the vinyl.

Wrapping the Front Bumper

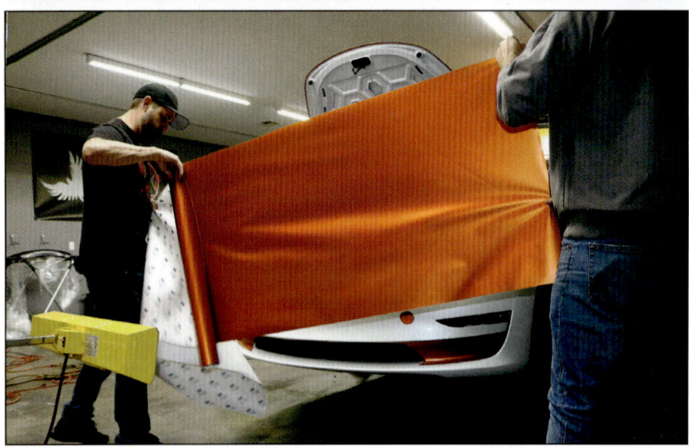

1 *Turn on the heat lamp while unrolling the bumper piece to allow plenty of time for the lamp to warm up.*

2 *The two-person approach is a preferred method of laying the front bumper piece.*

3 *With the backing peeled from the vinyl, begin to heat the middle section by placing it in front of the lamp.*

4 Once the material is heated, approach the vehicle and tack the middle section to the bumper. The installer on the right will tack the rest of the driver's side of the bumper and move to the middle section, whereas the installer on the left keeps the passenger-side vinyl off the bumper for now.

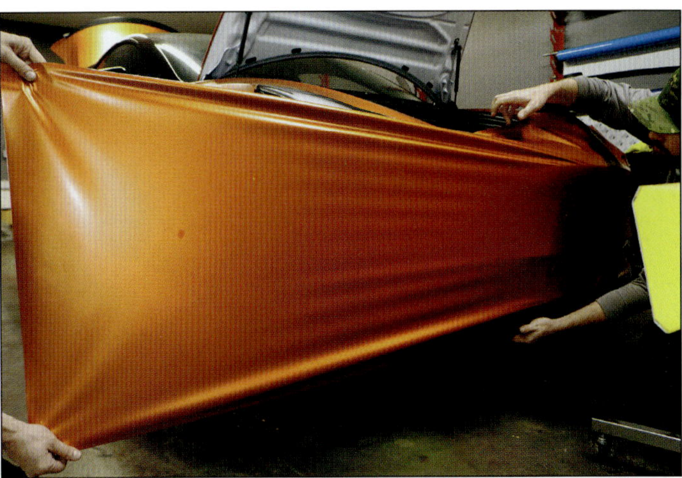

5 Using two people, pull the vinyl tight and position it while focusing only on the middle section of the bumper. The piece should be cut large enough to allow 5 to 6 inches of excess material at both the top and bottom of the panel.

6 As the installer at the end of the piece pulls the piece horizontally, the installer in the middle of the bumper stretches vertically by pulling at the top and bottom of the film.

7 Both installers are focusing on the location of the wrinkles, and they are applying tension accordingly to get the vinyl to lay smooth.

8 Continue around the curve and make sure that the vinyl goes down flat.

9 *Do not forget to move the heat lamp as you get closer to the end of the bumper. Always heat sections and then stretch as you work toward the end of the panel.*

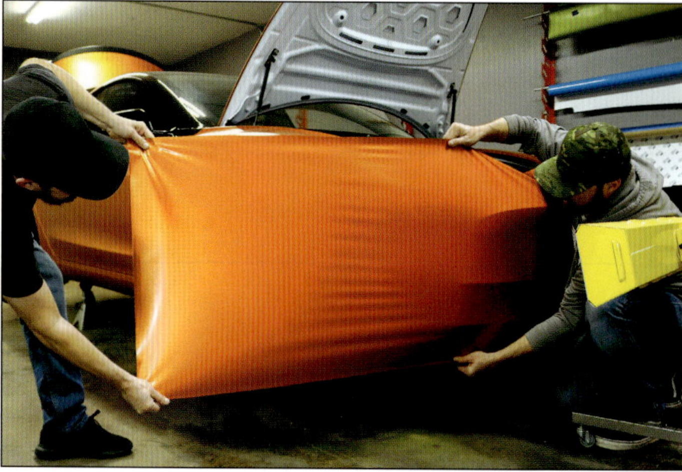

10 *Both installers need to work in unison, as each one helps the other apply tension.*

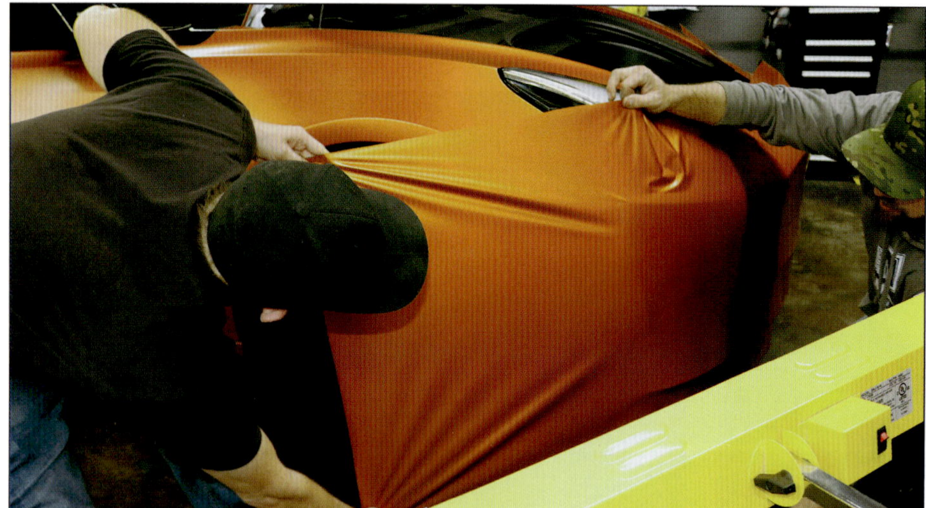

11 *The corner of the bumper requires a little extra heat, so stop stretching and let the lamp heat up the piece as you keep it still and lifted off the car.*

12 *The wrap is finished on the passenger's side of the front bumper installation. Repeat these steps to lay the driver's side and complete the initial front bumper application.*

Position the vinyl and only focus on the middle section of the bumper. The piece should be cut large enough to allow 5 to 6 inches of excess material at both the top and bottom of the panel.

Have one of the installers wrap his or her half of the vinyl around the bumper and lightly tack it to his or her end of the bumper. The other installer should hold their side just above the surface and supply tension to the piece while the first installer works toward them from the middle point of the panel.

During the installation, both installers use a combination of heat and tension to create a smooth surface in the vinyl needed for install. The installer at the far edge of the bumper applies outward tension while the installer working from the middle grips the top and bottom edges of the vinyl to create tension vertically.

After the middle portion of the bumper has been laid, the installer will reach the area where the panel begins to curve and bend it toward the fender. Use a good amount of heat and have both installers continue to create the same opposing forces of tension that they used to stretch the vinyl smoothly around the corner and out to the edge of the panel.

Repeat these steps and begin at the middle of the bumper to install the opposite side of the panel. Once both sides of the panel are laid, the vinyl should be virtually wrinkle free. You can now begin applying pressure with the squeegee and complete the installation process as described in Chapter 7.

Trunk Application

The trunk of a vehicle can pose a few difficult areas for a vinyl wrap

The rear Lexus emblem needs to be removed before the trunk install. Use adhesive remover to help loosen the adhesive left behind from the emblem.

installer. Here are a few tips and tricks to pull off an amazing-looking panel.

First, remove the license plate and license plate frame. Any emblems located on the panel must to be removed. See the disassembly portion of this chapter for steps on how to do so.

Use a general adhesive remover on that area prior to cleaning and make sure that all adhesive from the residue has been removed. If there is a rear spoiler located on the trunk, remove it along with any adhesive it may leave behind. Lastly, remove the taillights.

Examine the panel and envision your approach. If there is a drastic recess around the license plate area, consider placing an inlay in that area prior to laying the panel. Examine the bend in the trunk where the panel transitions from horizontal to a vertical surface.

If the bend is abrupt, you may want to wrap the trunk in two separate pieces and use the natural body line of the bend to position a seam. Always build from the bottom up to hide the seam. Refer to the seams section discussed in Chapter 7 for steps on how to do so.

Remove the remaining adhesive by using a plastic razor blade. These are inexpensive and is usually purchased in a pack of 100. They scrape away the adhesive without damaging the paint.

Once the trunk has been cleaned and prepped, use a hooking post to make the initial installation easier.

Most trunks can be wrapped in one piece, but to accomplish this you need two installers. With the installers standing on either side of the trunk, remove the adhesive, heat the vinyl, stretch the vinyl in a horizontal direction, and apply the material to the area of the bend, wrapping toward the bottom of the vertical portion of the trunk. Next, heat the horizontal surface of the panel and lightly stretch upward to complete the panel. You are now ready to apply pressure with a squeegee and continue the installation.

Inlaying the License Plate Area

1 *There are some high-tension corners around the rear license plate area. This top corner is one of them.*

2 *This bottom corner is another high-tension area. Install an inlay in these areas.*

3 *Notice the knifeless tape along the body line. This provides a nice clean cut once the inlay has been laid over it.*

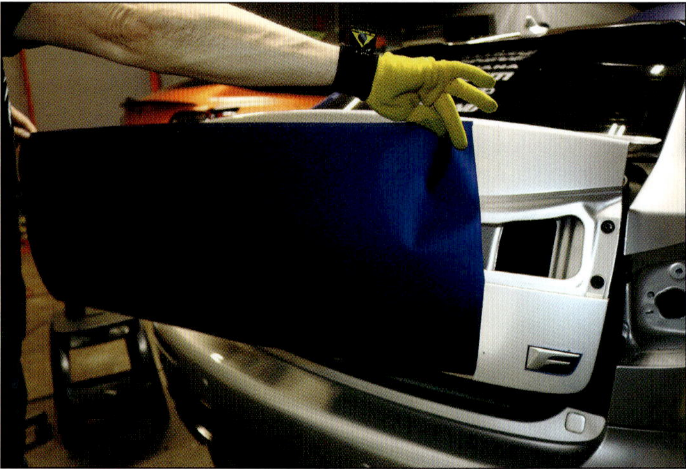

4 *Mock up the vinyl with the backing still attached to ensure that the piece will fit properly.*

5 *Peel the backing to the halfway point.*

6 *Place the first half of the inlay onto the vehicle.*

7 *With the vinyl attached to the vehicle, continue to remove the rest of the backing.*

8 *Keep this side of the vinyl off the vehicle to decrease tension.*

9 *Using the wrap glove, begin at the middle of the piece and work toward the left corner.*

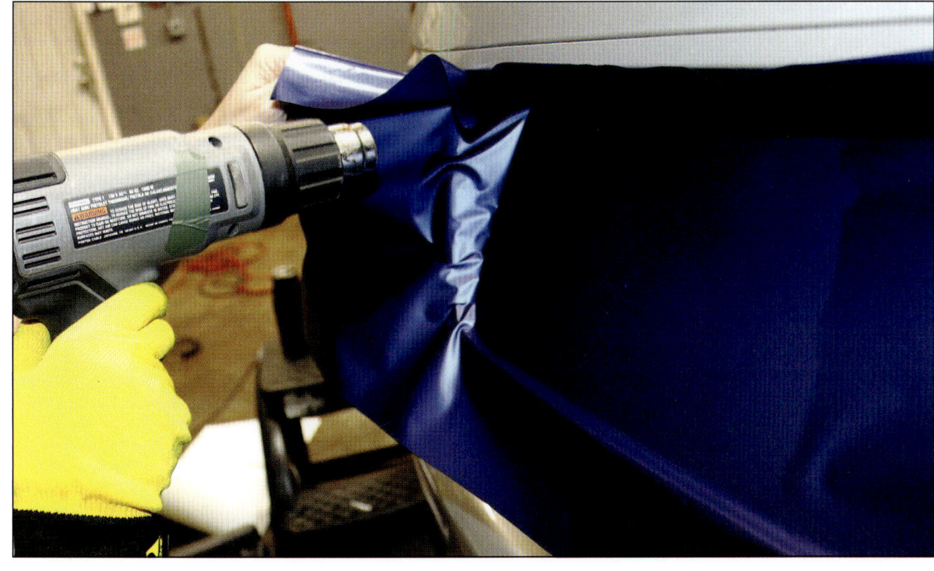

10 *Heat the corner while keeping the vinyl lifted.*

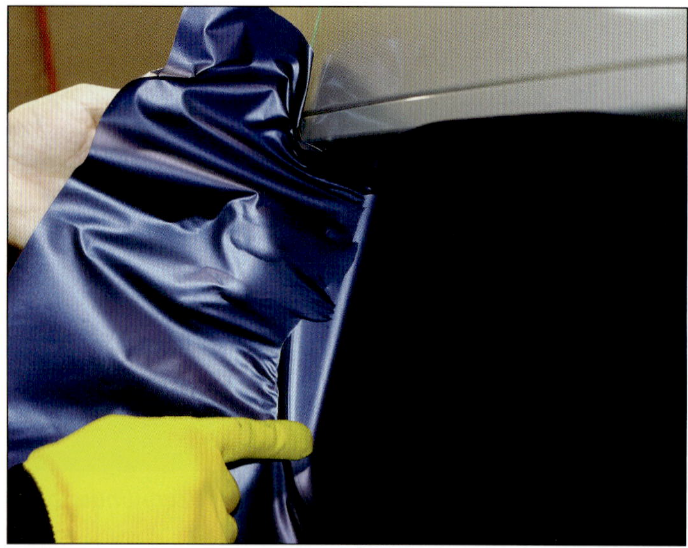

11 *Once heated, feed the corner of the vinyl down to the car.*

12 *Continue feeding the top of the corner and heat occasionally as needed.*

13 *The corners of the inlay have been completed.*

14 *Finish the corner at the right-hand side of the inlay.*

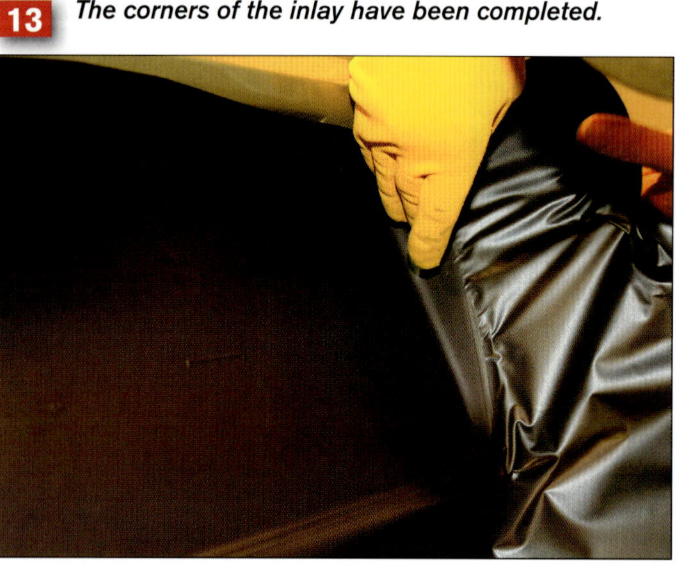

15 *Lift when needed to release air pockets.*

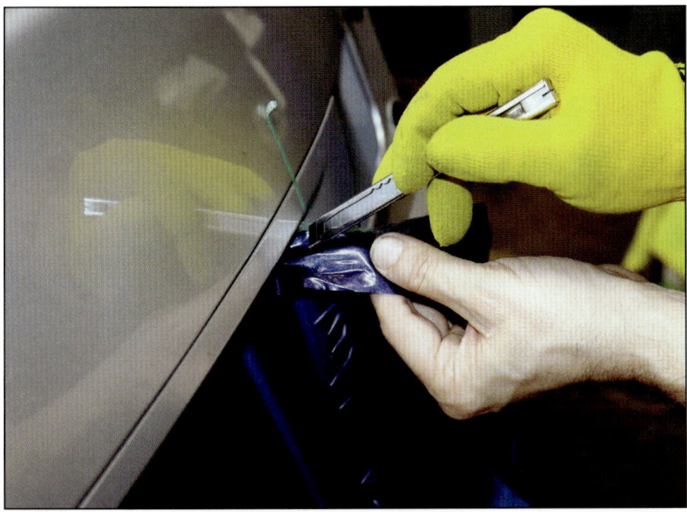

16 *Using your blade, create a 1/2-inch slit into the vinyl to create a starting point to run the knifeless string through.*

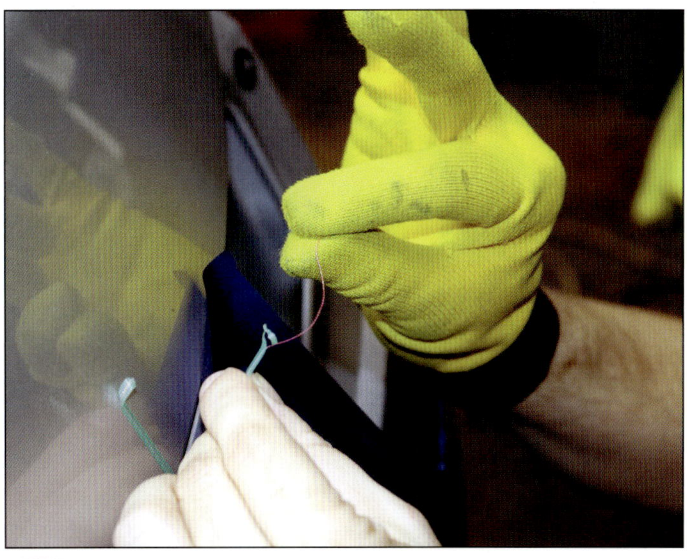

17 *Separate the string from the tape.*

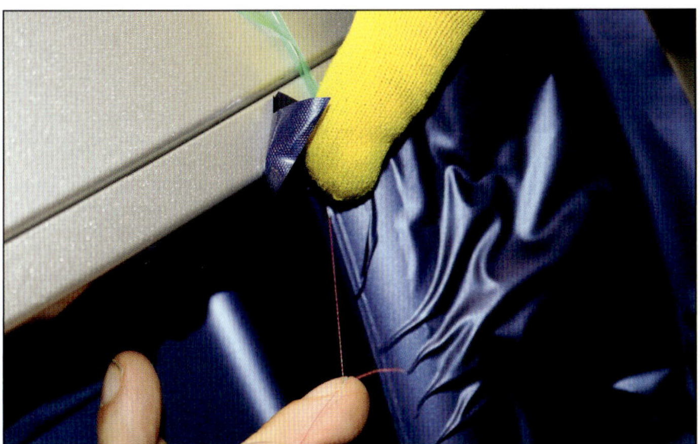

18 *Place your thumb over the area where the knifeless cut begins to prevent the vinyl from making a jagged cut.*

19 *Begin pulling the string. Notice the angle.*

20 *Keep a good amount of consistent tension while rounding the corner to ensure a clean cut.*

21 *Begin removing the excess vinyl.*

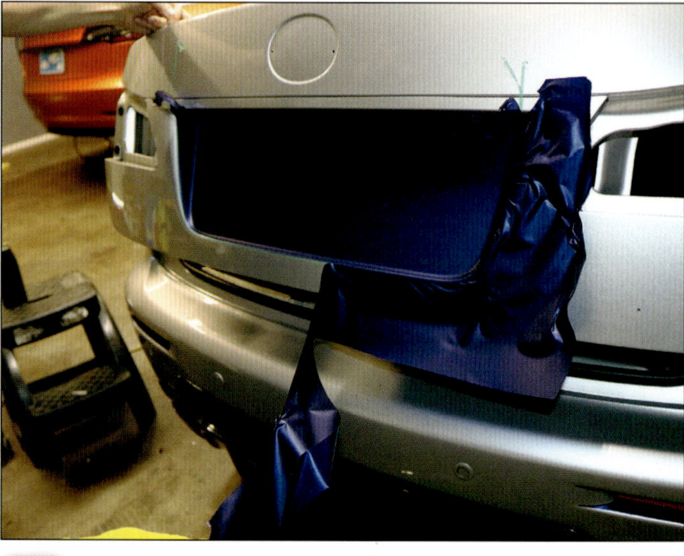

22 *The vinyl peels away easily.*

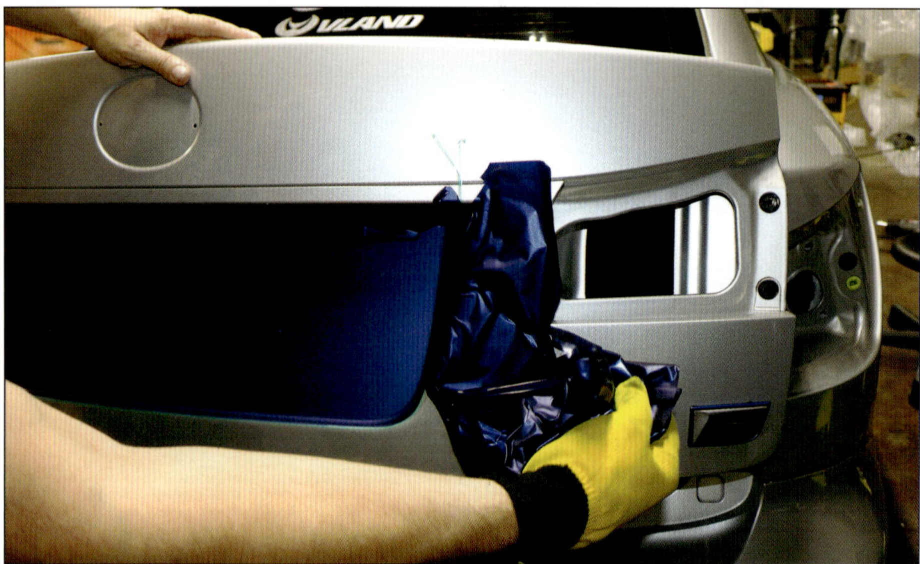

23 *The cut line that was left behind looks straight and clean.*

24 *This is the finished inlay. Lay another round of knifeless tape around the edge of this piece to prepare for laying the rest of the trunk vinyl over the top of it.*

Vinyl Wrapping the Trunk Lid

1 With the trunk piece cut, begin to peel the backing.

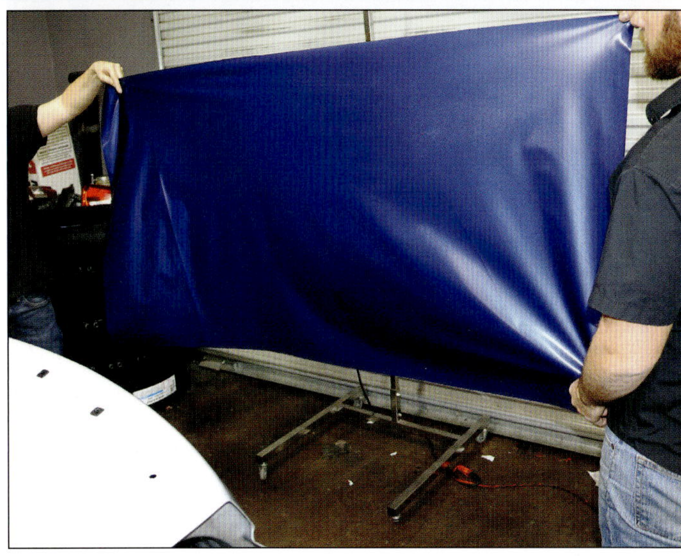

2 Heat the vinyl in front of the heat lamp once the backing is completely removed. When a panel contains a drastic curve, such as this one, be sure to heat the vinyl thoroughly so that it can stretch as needed.

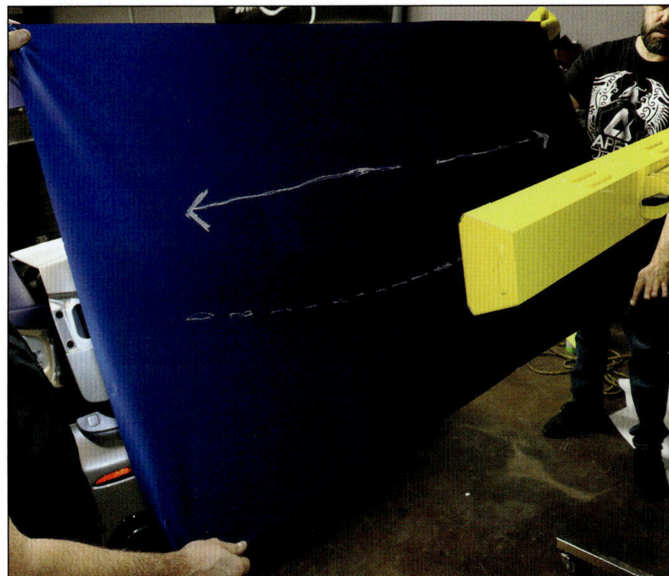

3 We used a vinyl-safe pen to place markings on the panel to outline how the initial lay would go down. The two solid lines toward the top designate the direction of the stretch between the two installers. The initial stretch is important on this panel because we are dealing with both the curvature of the back end of the trunk and the drastic angle after the curve as the back of the trunk turns downward. The dotted line below the other two lines indicates where the vinyl should hit the back curved section of the panel.

4 Be patient and wait for the entire piece to be heated. Hover the piece a few inches above the car and make sure the vinyl is lined up in a way that fully covers all four corners of the trunk. Once the coverage is verified, it is time to initialize the stretch.

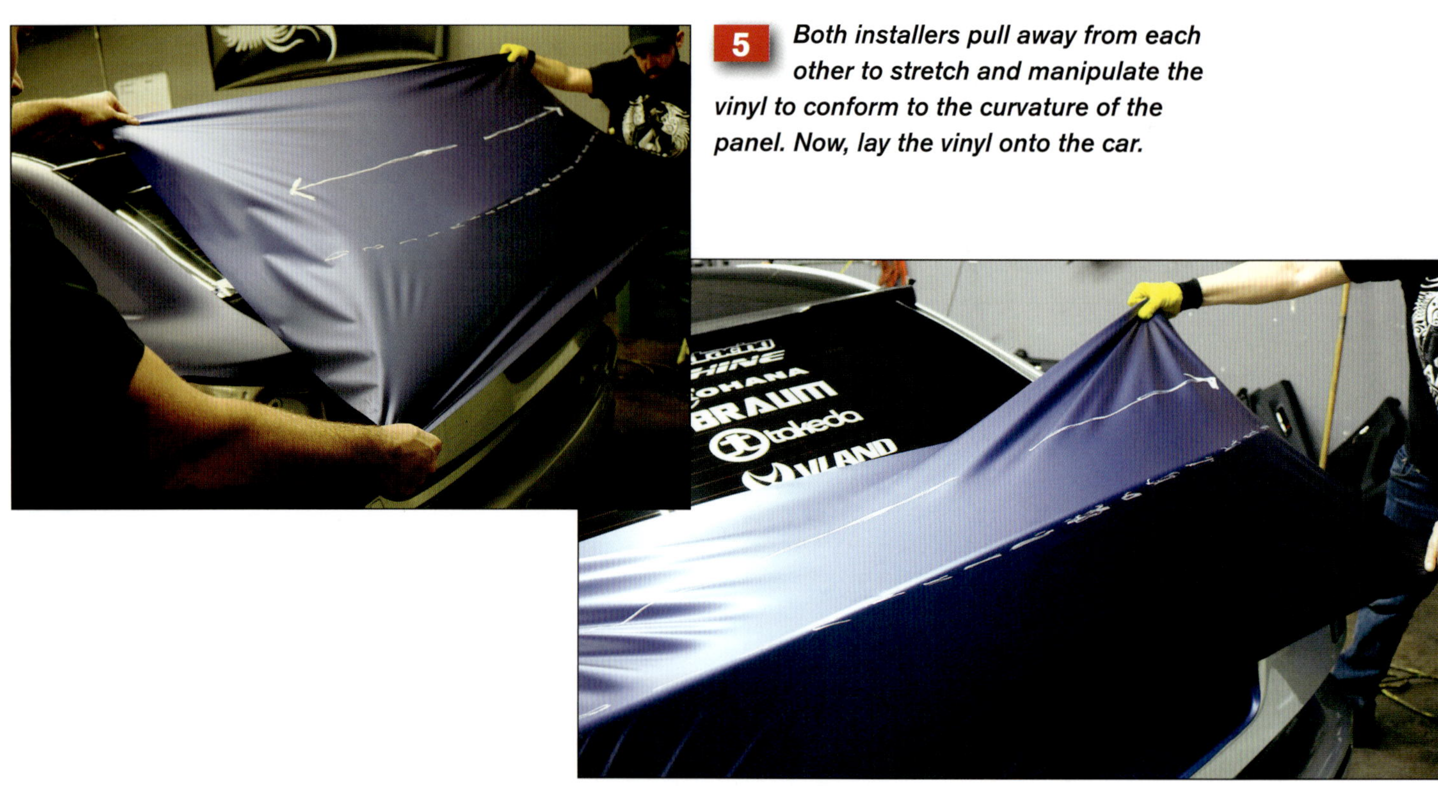

5 Both installers pull away from each other to stretch and manipulate the vinyl to conform to the curvature of the panel. Now, lay the vinyl onto the car.

6 Lift up the back two corners. Stretch outward toward the back glass. Do not worry too much about the wrinkles for now. Just make sure there's tension on the piece as it is applied to the glass.

7 With one hand, lift the rear corner of the vinyl off the car and move down slightly, heating out the wrinkles in that section. Begin at the top of the wrinkles and heat downward. They will slowly turn smooth.

8 Now that the vinyl is smooth, lay it back down onto the vehicle.

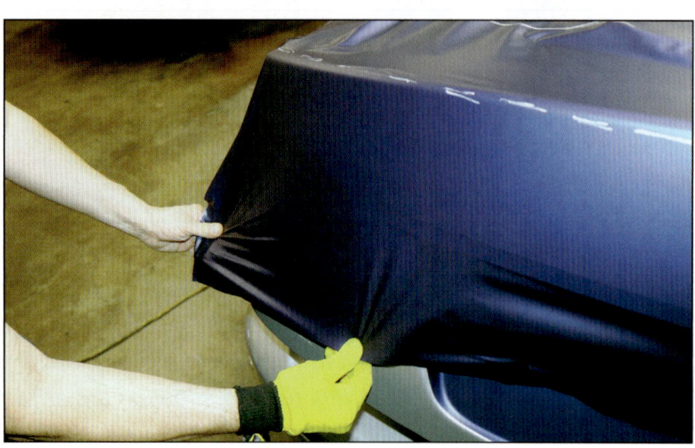

9 Lift the piece at the top of the trunk where the wrinkles are located.

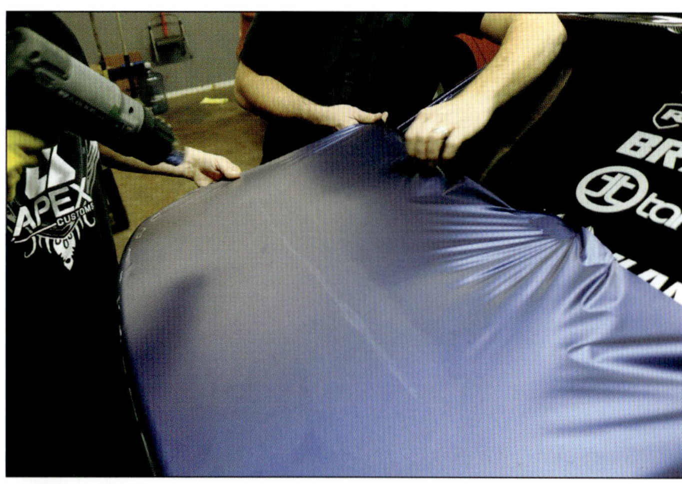

10 While keeping the tension on the vinyl, pull the piece toward the front of the vehicle, and heat out the wrinkles until it is smooth.

11 Applying pressure with a squeegee, begin in the middle and work toward the outer edge of the trunk.

12 Repeat the previous steps and heat out the wrinkles at the bottom corner of the trunk.

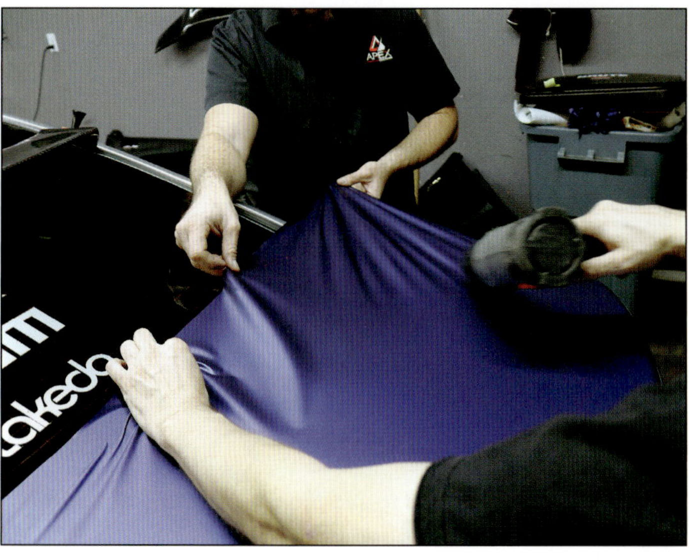

13 Heat the wrinkles at the top of the trunk to remove them.

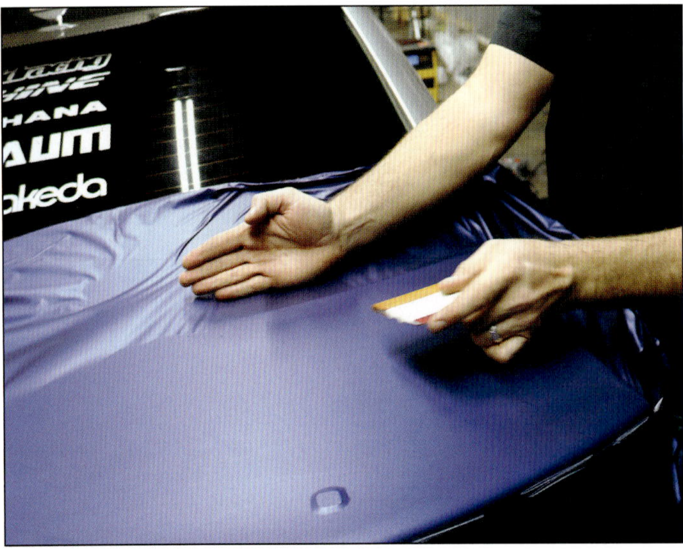

14 *Begin at the middle of the trunk and work outward.*

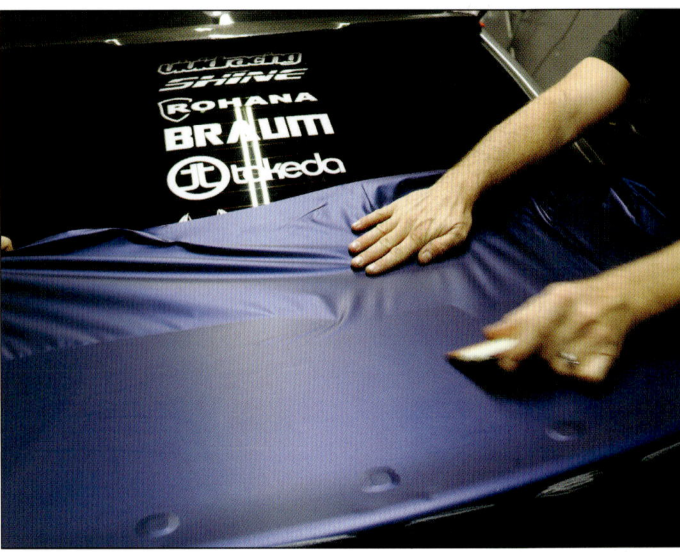

15 *Use a little heat from the heat gun on these wrinkles to smooth them out if needed.*

16 *Now, focus on getting the top of the trunk installed. Lift the area that shows wrinkles and with one hand.*

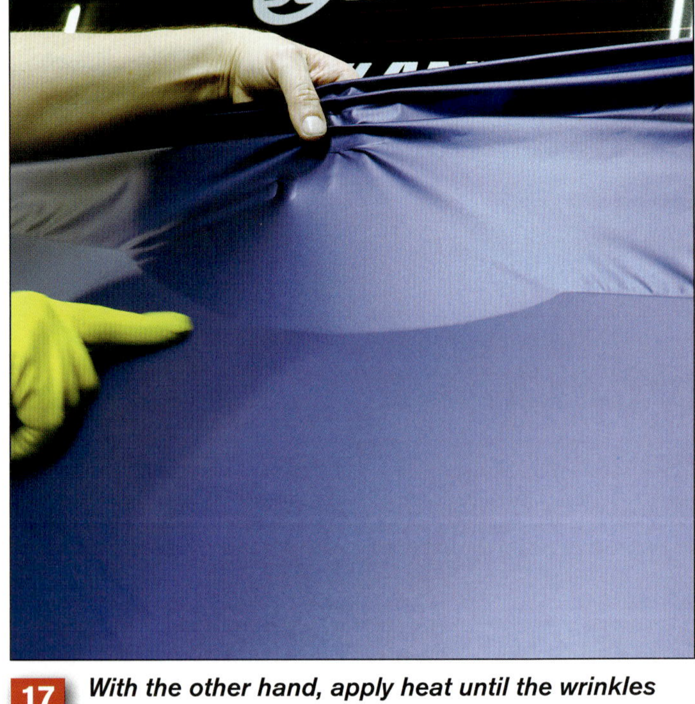

17 *With the other hand, apply heat until the wrinkles diminish.*

18 *On this particular trunk, there is a small indention where the Lexus badge is located.*

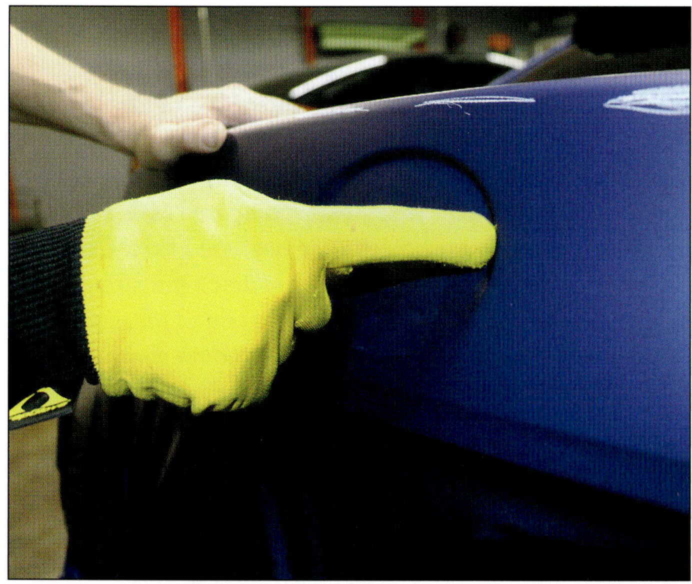

19 *Using a wrap glove, press firmly and run your finger around the indention.*

20 *If there's a tiny pocket of trapped air, you may need to create a small hole with the tip of a blade to let the air escape.*

21 *Continue applying pressure to the remainder of the panel. Once the entire piece has been laid, trim your edges, open the trunk, and complete tucking the wrap.*

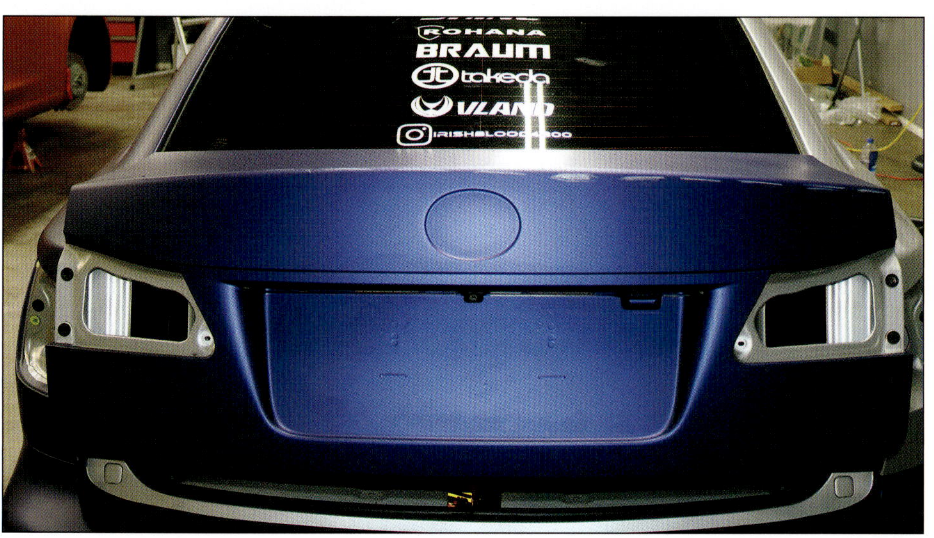

22 *Once that is done, give the panel a good post heat and move on to the next.*

Having areas free from dirt is essential for vinyl application. Dirt loves to hide beneath weatherstripping in instances such as the area at the top of the windshield. Pull back the weatherstripping and clean the area underneath. Be careful not to damage the weatherstripping when it is pulled back. Weatherstripping can take a beating in the sun and can become fragile over the years. Use a pick tool or squeegee to carefully pull back the stripping and get underneath. This is where the end of the vinyl will be tucked so no paint color will show. Hiding vinyl underneath weatherstripping is a must to get a perfect wrap.

When prepping a roof for vinyl installation, pay close attention to the dirt and grime that can hide inside the sunroof area. Start the cleaning process by opening the sunroof and start with this area first. It is often the dirtiest spot on the panel and sometimes is overlooked. If this section is not cleaned, the dirt will work against the adhesive and prevent it from sticking to the vehicle.

The roof rails are hard or soft plastic trim pieces located between the roof and the pillars. These are typically easy to remove and will make these areas much easier to wrap without the obstacle. Remove them before prepping the vehicle.

Once the roof rails have been removed, there will likely be dirt and debris in this area. This Toyota Tundra was less than a year old when the photo was taken. It does not take long for dirt to build up in this area. Thoroughly clean these valleys to avoid getting dirt trapped between the film and surface of the vehicle.

Roof Application

The roof of any vehicle has several areas that can trap dust. The cleaning phase may take a little more time and effort before you are ready to start your installation.

Lift the weatherstripping along the top of the front and rear window and clean underneath. If the vehicle is equipped with a sunroof, open it and make sure that all of the areas inside, including the tracks that the glass uses to retract, are clean and clear of debris.

Some models will also have trim pieces on the driver's side and passenger's side of the roof that run lengthwise on the panel. Remove them and clean underneath. There is often a fair amount of trapped dirt in these areas, so clean both valleys.

Lastly, if there is an antenna on the roof, the best-case scenario is to remove it. If the antenna cannot be removed in a timely manner, the installation can still take place with the antenna intact.

Once the cleaning process has been completed, it is now time to install the roof. Remember, when cutting the material, allow approximately 5 to 6 inches of extra vinyl on all four sides of the piece. Because the roof has so many areas where dirt may be hiding, refrain from lifting too many times during the install. To achieve this, a two-person back-roll method is highly recommended. First, lay the film with the backing still on onto the surface of the roof panel.

If you are wrapping a modern vehicle, chances are good that an antenna will be located on the roof. The easiest way to wrap panels like these is to remove the antenna and get it out of your way. However, if you are unable to do so, the next best way is to precut an area out of the vinyl before laying it on the roof.

Always prep and clean the panel prior to install.

Vinyl Wrapping the Roof

1 *Pull about 20 inches of backing off the material and lift that part of the vinyl straight up at a 90-degree angle.*

2 *Move the backing underneath the piece toward the front of the car.*

3 While lifting the material straight up at a 90-degree angle, slide the backing underneath the film and pull it toward the front of the vehicle.

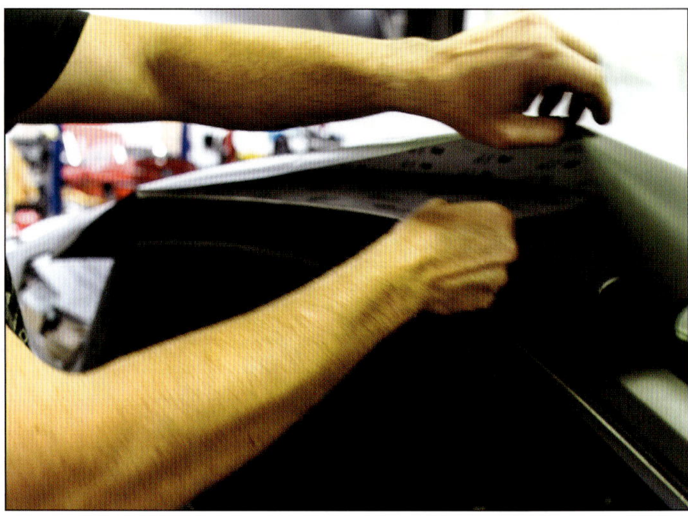

4 Lift the vinyl and then grab and pull the free piece of backing.

5 Both installers should have a grip on the backing and keep a slight amount of tension in between them.

6 Keep pulling until the backing is toward the front of the vehicle.

7 Completely remove the rest of the backing.

8 Remove the wrinkles at the front of car.

9 Lift the material and create tension. Once most of the wrinkles disappear, lay the vinyl back down to the surface.

10 *Repeat the same steps to remove the wrinkles in the vinyl at the rear of the roof.*

Starting at the rear of the vehicle, with one installer on either side of the vehicle, peel approximately 20 inches of the film from the backing. Lift the material straight up at a 90-degree angle, slide the backing underneath the film, and pull the backing toward the front of the vehicle. Continue pulling the rest of the backing from the piece.

Tightly tack the loose material to the rear window and have each

Measure the distance from the rear of the antenna to the rear of the roof and add 5 inches. Record and label this measurement as "antenna rear." In this example, that measurement is 9½ inches. This is where the back of the antenna will start on the piece of film. The 5 extra inches will provide a nice amount of excess material at the rear of the panel.

Measure the width of the antenna at the rear. This section of the vinyl will be slightly smaller than the antenna itself, so subtract a 1/2 inch from this measurement. Record the measurement as "bottom width." In this example, it is 1¾ inches.

Measure the length of the antenna. This measurement will be about a 1/2 inch shorter than the antenna. Record and label the measurement. In this example, it is 3½ inches.

Next, get a measurement for the width of the front of the antenna. Usually, the width of most antennas is narrower toward the front. In this example, the measurement is 1¼ inches. Make sure to label and record the number.

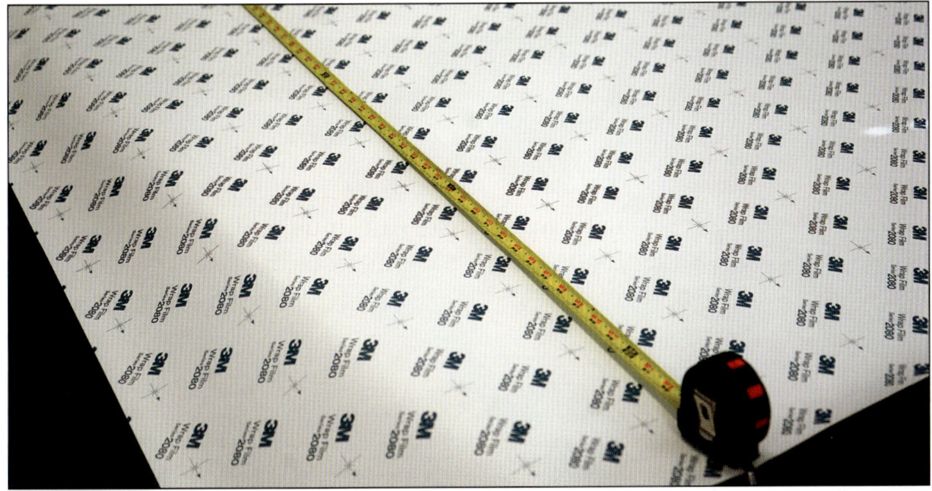

This section will illustrate the steps needed to cut a roof panel with a precut area for the antenna to slip through. Begin by laying the vinyl out on the cut table and measure the length of the film needed to cover the roof. Remember to cut the length 5 or 6 inches longer than the panel at both the front and rear of the panel.

Go to the bottom edge of the film and measure to find its center point. The total width of the film in this photo is 60 inches, so measure to see where the 30-inch point lies. Place a mark to keep track of the spot.

Now, find out where the rear of the antenna will land on the vinyl. Using the rear antenna measurement (in this case 9½ inches), measure the distance up from the bottom edge of the film. Mark the spot to keep track of the measurement.

With a blade, cut a line through the vinyl that equals the measurement of the length of the antenna at the rear. Make sure the incision goes all the way through the backing and the vinyl.

installer put his or her hands under the film so that he or she can get a firm grip on the backing. While each installer grips the backing, walk and pull the backing toward the front of the car until it has been completely removed.

With both installers still on either side of the vehicle, lift the material at the front and rear of the panel to make slight adjustments, and use tension between both installers to get the material to lay smooth on the surface. The goal at this point is to keep adjustments to a minimum. Keep in mind that every time the material is lifted, dust and debris can slip in.

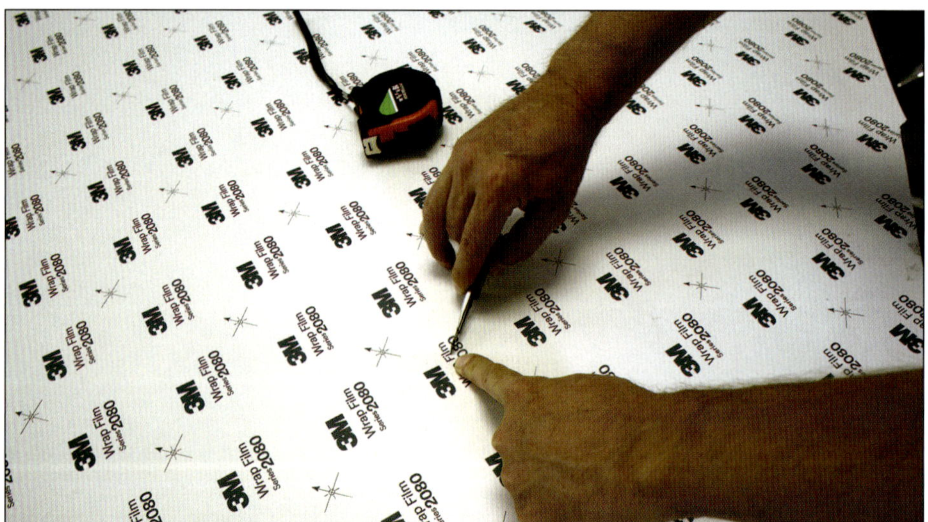

Find the measurement recorded for the length of the antenna and measure to find where the top of the antenna will be. Check your measurements to find the width of the front of the antenna and cut a line for that width.

Roof Antenna

If you are installing a roof that includes an antenna and decided to wrap the panel without removing the antenna, perform a precut in the material to create a hole in the vinyl for the antenna to slip through during the install. It will require a few more steps as you cut the piece, but it's not extremely difficult once you understand the process.

You need to get five different measurements before you can cut the roof piece.

First, measure the length of the roof from windshield to rear window. Do not forget to add 5 inches at each end to provide extra room to work with during the install. Write down the measurement and label that number something like "roof length" to reference later.

Now, measure the distance between the rear of the antenna and where the rear glass begins. Add 5 inches to that number and label it "antenna rear."

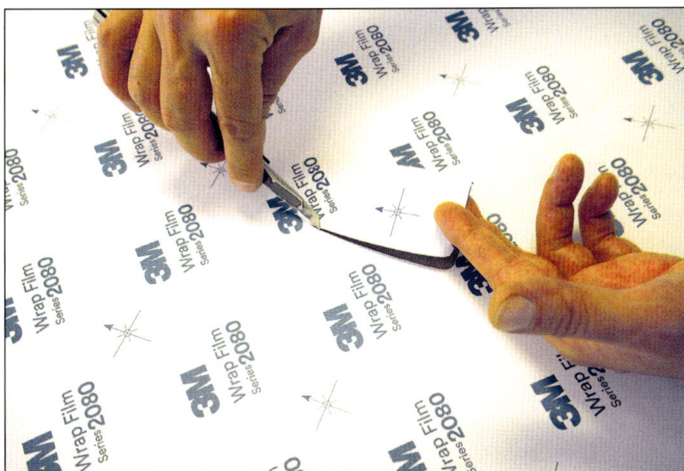

Cut a line through the vinyl on both sides of the antenna to connect the front to the rear.

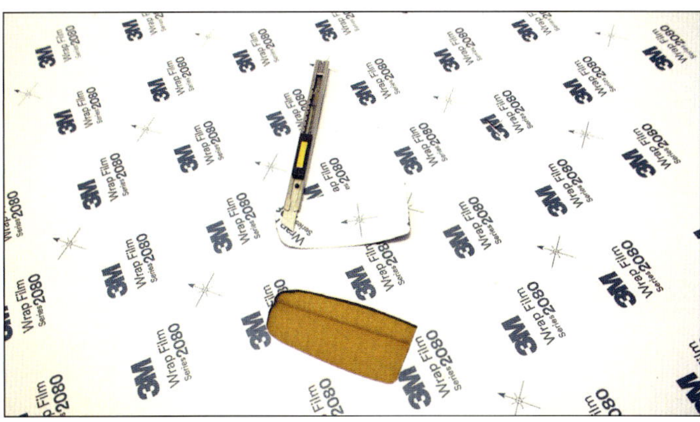

Remove the piece that has been completely cut out. This piece of vinyl will be used to wrap the roof. The precut area will line up with the antenna on the roof perfectly and will make the roof install a lot less difficult.

Peel the backing and lay the vinyl while lining up the precut portion of the film with the antenna. Don't begin installing at the front of the roof opposite the antenna because there will likely be too much tension when applying that area. Instead, start with the antenna area. Use your fingers to lift the film where it is touching the vinyl to fully release all tension. With a heat gun, apply a little heat and work the vinyl into the antenna on all four sides. Finish the area around the antenna first, and the rest of the panel will go down smoothly.

Next, measure only the width of the antenna itself at its rear. Subtract a half inch from that measurement, write it down, and label it "bottom width."

Now, measure the length of the antenna and subtracting a half inch from the number and write it down.

Lastly, take the measurement of the width at the top of the antenna, subtract a 1/4 inch, and write it down.

Once you have these measurements, cut the piece. Place the film on a cut table and roll out the appropriate length. Cut the length of the film you need off the roll.

Typically, you will use the 60-inch width provided, so do not worry about trimming anything off the sides. Move to the bottom of the piece that you just cut and find the center. Using the number for "antenna rear," measure that distance up from the bottom edge of your piece. This is where the bottom of the antenna will be.

Find the measurement for "bottom width," and cut a line in the material. Measure the antenna length to find where the top of the antenna will be, and make the next cut be the width at the top of the antenna.

With a blade, cut out the width for the top of the antenna and connect the top and bottom by cutting both sides out last. Remove the piece you just cut out. The antenna precut is done, and the material is ready to be installed.

Use the same back-roll method that was described earlier. Begin at

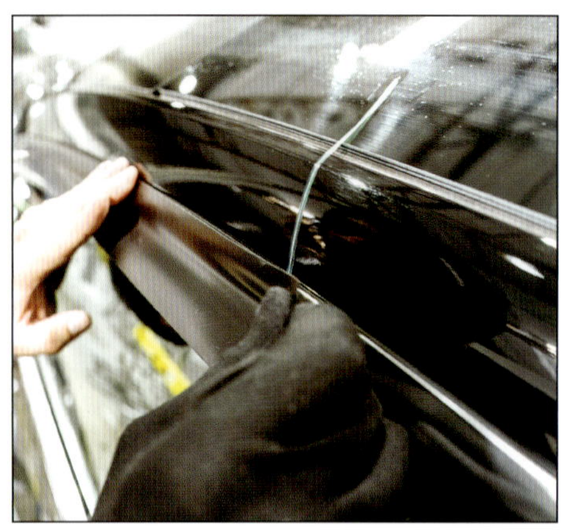

the rear of the vehicle as you begin the back roll, and line up the area that you have precut with the antenna on the roof. Let the antenna slip through the hole. Before you go any further, make sure that everything is lined up and no factory paint is showing.

Continue the rest of the back roll, peel the rest of the backing, and get the entire piece laid smoothly onto to the roof. Get all the film around the antenna area first before applying pressure and continue with the installation. Since this location has the potential to build a lot of tension, if it is done before all other areas, there's a better chance of avoiding any unwanted ugly tension lines. Lift the material off the antenna to release tension. Use a little heat to shrink the material and squeegee all the vinyl to all edges of the antenna. After all the vinyl has been laid around the antenna, continue installing the rest of the panel.

Trim Application

There is a large demand to cover a vehicle's chrome trim pieces with vinyl wrap. It is typically referred to as a "de-chrome" or "chrome delete," and it usually uses a matte, satin, or gloss black vinyl. It can transform any vehicle and give it an amazing look. Chrome trim can be found in various areas on a vehicle, and it is important to know which pieces can be wrapped and which cannot.

The trim around the windows on both sides of the vehicle is almost always a great candidate for vinyl wrap. Seldom are there be any complications on these areas. There are only a few steps to make things go smoothly.

On a long chrome trim piece such as this, the installer is using two strips of material to save film. One long continuous piece will provide the best look. If you decide to use two pieces, make the seam land in a natural spot on the trim, such as in line with the pillar as shown here. This makes it easier to hide and not look out of place.

Make the seam follow the same angle as the pillar shown here. Remember, the key is to make the seam look natural and well hidden. Another way to hide the seam is to start working from the rear of the vehicle so that the piece located above the front door (an area usually viewed the most) will overlap the rear piece so the seam will face away from the passenger's regular sightline.

Vinyl Wrapping Trim

1 *Wrapping the chrome trim pieces on a vehicle is an easy way to upgrade its appearance. Begin with the piece farthest to the rear and work toward the front of the vehicle. The front pieces of vinyl will overlap those at the rear and the seams will face away from the driver's view to give the installation a professional appearance.*

2 *After the surface of the trim has been installed, move to the edge, lift the vinyl, and use the hard plastic side of the squeegee to tuck the vinyl into the bottom of the trim. Any area that is not completely covered by the vinyl will result in a poor installation. By using the lift-and-tuck method, no sliver of chrome will be left uncovered when the excess vinyl is trimmed.*

3 *This rear trim piece is fully wrapped after all of the excess vinyl has been trimmed. The vinyl has been tucked into the rubber molding that runs along the inner section of the trim. This will give the installation a clean, professional look.*

4 *A seam is added here where the next piece of vinyl wrap overlaps the piece that was just installed. The location of the seam is important to make it look as natural as possible. In this example, there's a natural break to follow in the trim piece. However, if a piece of trim is continuous, have the seam follow a natural line, such as the one coming up from the window, so that the seam will not look out of place.*

5 *Before installing the next piece of vinyl, place a strip of knifeless tape along the edge of the previous piece of vinyl as shown in the photo. This will provide a nice clean line without having to use a blade.*

6 *Begin installing the second piece of vinyl by placing it an inch or two over the edge of the previous piece. Do not forget to thoroughly clean each piece of trim just prior to laying the vinyl.*

7 *The far end of the chrome trim does not provide a natural break in the piece. We will add a seam that follows the line of the pillar located directly below it, which will give the installation a professional appearance.*

8 *After the vinyl has been installed, tucked, and trimmed, pull the string from the knifeless tape to remove the excess material at the far edge of the vinyl.*

9 *Notice how the cut made with the knifeless tape follows the same angle as the pillar located below it. This provides a professional-looking seam when the next piece is laid and cut following the same angle.*

10 *The chrome door handles, the trim around the windows, and the trim below the side mirror on this Tesla Model 3 have been wrapped in satin black vinyl. No matter the vehicle, an upgrade such as this will create an amazing modern look.*

Cleaning

We have already discussed the importance of cleaning, but it must be mentioned again because it is still the single most important step.

That being said, a straightedge with a sliding blade attached is a useful tool to have when cutting pieces of vinyl for window trim. The goal is to cut the vinyl in a way that gives you a piece that is taller than the chrome trim you are wrapping with a straightedge at the top and bottom of the piece. Use that straight cut during installation to align it onto to the trim exactly where you want it to be in a way that will only require one cut along the bottom of the trim. This will cut the workload in half.

Plotter

If you have access to a plotter, it is a great way to obtain that straight edge. Most trim pieces fall under the 60-inch width of a roll of vinyl, which allows the installer to cut the film off the roll horizontally and save on cost.

However, some vehicles have a longer continuous trim piece over the top of the windows, and a decision must be made: cut the piece vertically off the roll (which can be expensive) or use two separate pieces of vinyl.

I usually leave it up to the client and price the job accordingly.

Two-Piece Application

If you choose to lay the panel in two pieces, here are a few pointers to get the best results.

First, decide where to put the seam. The best way is to look for a natural spot between the two windows. Select a position directly above a pillar or in line with the rear door.

Install a piece closer to the rear of the vehicle first so that the piece toward the front of the vehicle lays on top. This will make the seam more pleasing to the eye from the driver's point of view and will cancel out any wind drag.

Lastly, be consistent. Whatever choices are made on one side of the vehicle, mirror it on the other side. Inconsistencies will not go unnoticed and make the wrap installation look less professional.

Front of the Vehicle

Some of the more complex pieces in a chrome-delete project are located at the front of the vehicle, and often the grille is the most challenging.

In our years of experience, we found ways to tame the beast. Take a moment to inspect the piece and go over different approaches of how to proceed before you begin. Look for places where a seam will be inconspicuous. Be careful not to place too much tension inside recesses and curves. High tension can result in the wrap failing and lifting over time.

For example, take the style of the grille on the Lexus IS 350. Many owners of this vehicle prefer the chrome outer border wrapped in black vinyl. Doing this in one piece results in high tension inside the top two corners and can result in lifting over time. A piece on either side and one in the middle will alleviate the tension and offer greater longevity.

However, we also want the finished piece to look good, so placement of the seam is important. If we place the seam at either corner, it gives us an inconspicuous place to do so. This is important: if we wrap both side pieces and the top piece last, the seam will face the ground and away from our viewing angle. Clean, precise cuts will make the seam more pleasing to the eye, and mirroring the same angle on both sides will provide the consistency wanted from a professional install.

Another piece located at the front of the vehicle that people often like wrapped is the front splitter. Because these pieces are concave and follow the natural curve of the bumper, they pose some difficulty and can lift over time if not done by using the correct approach.

The secret to laying a piece with this shape is using the horizontal stretch during the initial lay. Do not lay the vinyl loose on a surface with this type of shape. Use a two-person approach, heat the vinyl, give it a slight stretch, and tightly lay the entire piece along the whole surface.

The idea behind this type of approach is to allow the vinyl to hug the surface of the splitter by wrapping it around the piece. By doing so, the chance of any lifting or fingering along the edges of the piece is greatly reduced.

Other areas that may require wrapping during a chrome delete project include smaller pieces, such as around the fog light areas and flat single pieces near the trunk. These are typically the easier pieces to wrap where minimal stretching is required. Pay attention to not leave any excess material around the corners and that all the edges are clean.

Final Touches

We covered every panel of the vehicle necessary to wrap and perform a full color change, including a full chrome delete. However, there are a few more items to discuss to ensure that all the hard work will last for years to come.

We have yet to cover one of the most important steps in wrapping a vehicle: the post heating process. Post heating enables the film to relax in high-tension areas, and if it is done immediately after the panel is wrapped, it will provide extra stability and help prevent the film from failing in those areas.

Another benefit to post heating is the way it is visible if there is an area in the film that has not been laid down to the surface with enough pressure. During the post-heating phase, these areas will form a bubble. Once cooled, it can be pressed back down to the vehicle to eliminate the issue.

To post heat a panel, wave the heat gun in a circular pattern approximately 4 to 5 inches from the surface in an even pattern over the entire panel. Pay close attention to the areas where the vinyl is under a greater amount of tension. Heat these high-tension areas for a few seconds using a circular motion with the gun, move the heat gun away from the surface for a few seconds, and heat the area again.

Never focus on one area with the heat gun for too long. Anything more than 5 or 6 seconds can damage the vinyl. Post heating every panel as soon as its completed is highly recommended. An additional final post heat over all panels after the entire vehicle has been wrapped is a good practice to ensure that no areas have been missed.

Reassembly

Finally, the reassembly process can begin. This procedure often takes more time than originally expected, so plan for it when working with deadlines. You can shave a lot of valuable time off this process if you were organized during disassembly.

Taking the effort to group nuts, bolts, and clips into plastic bags and labeling them according to location and parts will help. Other organization methods, such as using tape to mark pieces as "driver's side" or "passenger's side," will not only speed up your reassembly but also ensure that no parts go missing.

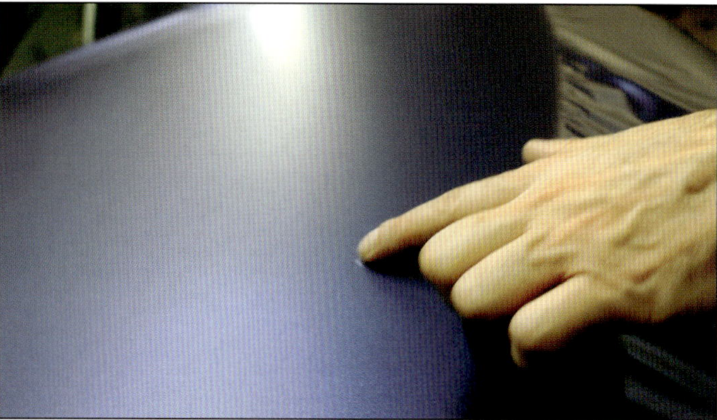

Even when panels are laid perfectly, small bubbles can still pop up. A flat panel laid flat can show a small bubble, especially after a post heat. The post heat excites the air molecules, which causes them to merge and bounce around to form a bubble.

Small bubbles can easily be pressed back down with a wrap glove. The pressure will cause the bubbles to find their quickest route out of the film through the air channels. Take care when pressing down the bubbles; larger ones can cause creases in the film. A crease in the film means that the whole panel must be re-layed. There is nothing to be said on the type of bubble and how easy it is to remove until you have enough experience.

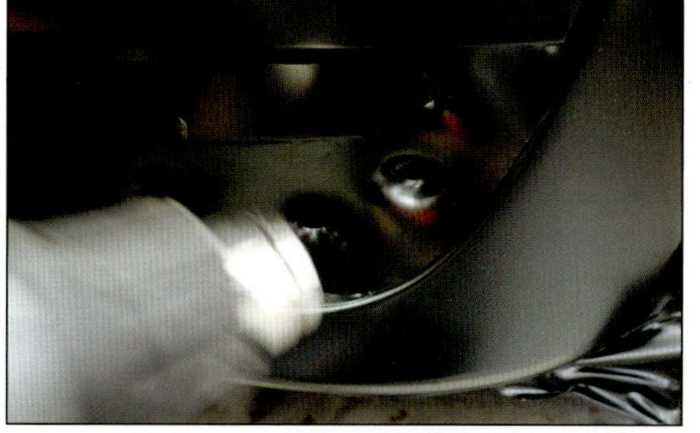

High-tension areas are the most likely candidates for problems. Complex curves and indentations are a breeding ground for problems. This is why these complex areas need to be focused on post heating. Bumpers are one of the most difficult areas to wrap because of the high number of high-tension areas. Heating these problem areas will allow any future issues to be addressed right away. Think of it as a test for your recently applied wrap.

The heat gun needs to be close enough to treat the film, yet far enough away not to burn it. Post heating is the process of applying heat over the film after it has been installed. This is done to get any of the air molecules that are visibly hiding to band together and form a bubble that can be addressed. It's better to remove a bubble pop-up now than a week later. If a bubble is treated right away, it's usually an easy fix. If a bubble exists for a week or two, the sun can bake off the adhesive that's not attached to the car, and it will be hard to stick back down.

When dissembling the vehicle, take the steps to make the reassembly process go as smoothly as possible. To make this happen, stay organized through the entire procedure. When working on a particular panel, keep all the hardware for that panel secured and labeled in a resealable plastic bag so that it doesn't go missing. Doing this for each panel will make reassembling the vehicle a much simpler task.

Vinyl Graphics Installation

There are many ways to transform the look of a vehicle, and applying graphics is one of them. Someone might want to add graphics to a vehicle for many reasons. Some may want to upgrade the look of the vehicle and give it a great custom look. Others find that it is an excellent way to promote their business and increase sales by adding a company logo, list of services, and/or contact information. No matter the goal, graphics can drastically change the look of any vehicle, interior wall, or storefront.

This chapter covers the steps before creating graphics, producing the graphics themselves, various installation techniques, and completing the project. Some additional steps must be taken when working in a professional setting, and the goal is to complete a specific project for a client. This entails ironing out design details and communicating with the client to give them the look that they envision.

If you are installing graphics on your own vehicle, you'll know firsthand the look for which you are going, but this chapter includes pointers to assist you as well.

Design Phase

It is important to know the precise year, make, and model of the vehicle with which you will be working. In a situation with a client, meet with them in person and see the vehicle firsthand. At this initial stage, discuss all aspects of the design, confirm the vehicle type, and take photos.

Photos of all four sides of the vehicle (front, rear, driver's side, and passenger's side) will be useful when it comes time to provide the client with various mockups of the design. This is also a perfect time to go over color schemes. Sample color books can be purchased from most vinyl manufacturers. They are inexpensive, and you can use them to show the client exactly what the actual color of the vinyl will look like.

This van has a bit of everything in the graphics arsenal. Graphics can be printed, plotted, or cut. This design uses OEM paint as part of the design. The white color is the van's paint, and the rest of the vehicle is wrapped. The front end of the vehicle and the yellow-and-black stripes are all printed graphics. The white numbers are a white film that has been plotted. There are many ways to produce a graphic like this. Many do this as a single print and then plot it. In this case, it also has cut decals applied over the printed material.

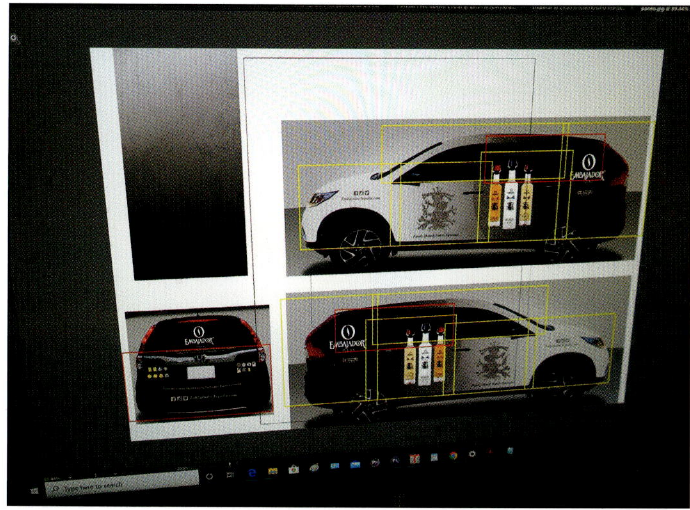

A mock-up can be done from a customer's vehicle picture or a template. BadWrap makes great design templates. Notice the boxes in this photo. This is where the graphic producer made the panels. The film is only 58 inches wide at its max, so work with the constraints of the film and what will work best for the install. When there are panels, there will be seams, so do your best to plan the panels so that the seams land in areas such as door lines.

A template is used to give the client an idea of what the vehicle will look like after the wrap is installed. Mock-ups can be made using many programs. There are so many programs that the number is changing daily. They vary in price from hundreds to thousands of dollars. At first, partner with someone to help with this side of the work. Try online freelance websites, such as upwork.com, for designers. They can help you get started in this business. Knowing design in the vinyl game is invaluable, so if there is one extra skill to learn, it's graphic design.

Walk around the vehicle with the client and find out details, such as the location and how large or small he or she wants the graphics. Guide the client away from obstacles, such as door handles, gas caps, or anything that may take away from the graphic and distort it in any way. For most people, it may be the first time they are getting graphics done, and as a professional installer, it is up to you to help them decide where the graphic will look its best. If the graphic is for a client's business, ask him or her to provide any artwork on file.

Established companies typically have a handful of files that they have used in the past, possibly while creating a website, business cards, or advertisements. Others may be starting out and ask for you to create something for them.

In any case, this early stage is an opportune time to find out what they may or may not have. If the client is looking for a custom design unrelated to any business or commercial project and wants to upgrade the look of his or her personal vehicle, he or she may already have an exact design in mind or may look to you for insight or ideas. It is always good to have something visual that you can both use as a reference when discussing the specifications of a particular design.

The internet is an excellent resource and offers a variety of images for projects. Often, a client can find the exact graphic that he or she wants, and other times you can use a picture of certain design as a starting point. In this case, discuss the areas of the design that the client likes as well as what he or she wants to change to suit his or her own style.

When this initial meeting concludes and you have a good grasp on the graphic that the client wants, you can begin the next phase of the design.

Mock-Ups, Adjustments, and Obtaining Final Approval

A picture says a thousand words, and we covered how showing a client a picture of a graphic can make communicating ideas much easier. The same holds true with the adjustment phase of any design.

Being able to show the client exactly what the graphic will look like prior to it being produced helps eliminate potential mistakes and avoid wasting time, material, and money.

Show the client what the graphic is going to look like but also show him or her what the actual graphic will look like on the vehicle. Many software programs allow you to upload photos of the owner's vehicle and position the graphics on the vehicle so that the client can see firsthand what the design will look like after the graphic has been installed.

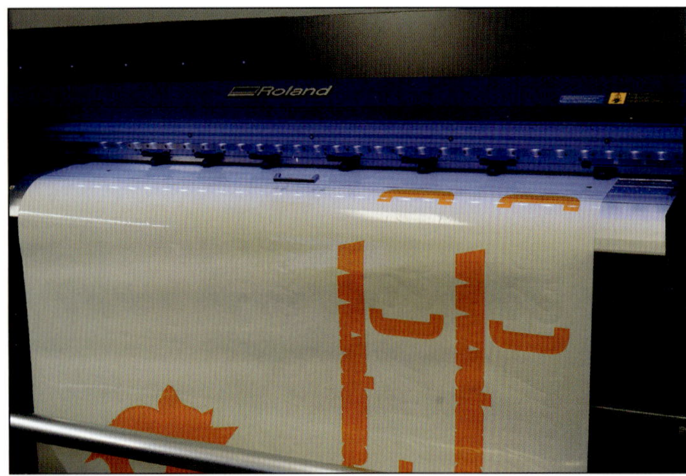

Many machines are used to produce graphics. Ours is a printer and a plotter in one, which means that it can both print and cut out the graphics. Between the print and the plot step, the material must be put through a laminator to seal and protect the print. After this is performed, load it back in the plotter. This graphic has been printed and laminated, and it is being cut, or plotted.

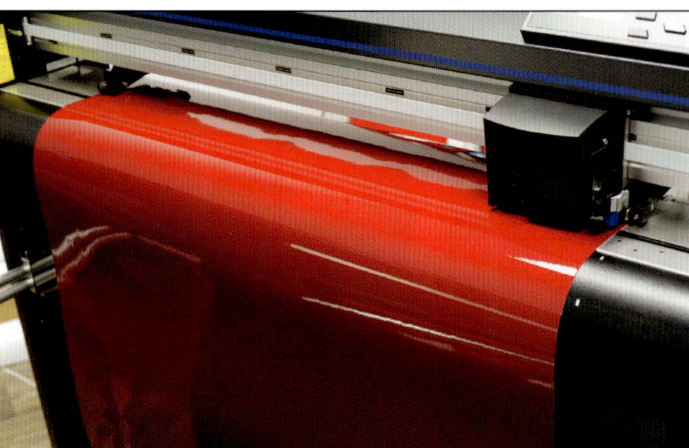

This is a plot-only machine. It is generally used for quick plot graphics of single-color materials. The design that tells which cuts need to be made is sent to the machine, and then the machine works its magic. Generally, this machine is great for plotting single-color graphics. We also use it to cut Clear Bra kits. Several companies, such as SunTek, make software for cutting out Clear Bra kits, bumpers, and hoods for all kinds of vehicle types.

Once the first mock-up is created, email it to the client and wait for their feedback. This method makes the entire adjustment phase easy and convenient, and the whole process can be handled without the client ever having to visit in person.

There are times when a certain design requires a few different mock-ups sent back and forth to the client. It is common for the client to request adjustments to the design or for some graphics to be moved to a different area of the vehicle. When the client has agreed on a final version of the design, get confirmation in writing that the client is happy with the design of the project. Then, move on to the next step, which is the phase where you create and produce the graphics to the agreed-upon specifications.

approved by the client that can be referenced to determine the colors to use, where each graphic will be placed on the vehicle, and the approximate size each graphic needs to be to cover the space on the vehicle shown in the design. Using this information, determine what areas of the vehicle need to be measured. Contact the client and schedule a time to measure the vehicle. This process can be done quickly and typically takes about 30 minutes to complete.

After the measurements are recorded, inform the client about the time that is required to produce and install the graphics as well as the amount of time you may have to

Production Phase

Now that the design has been completed, you have a final mock-up

Some simple cuts on a machine can turn into someone's unique custom project. This Corvette's graphics were created with a plotter, a design, and some hard work.

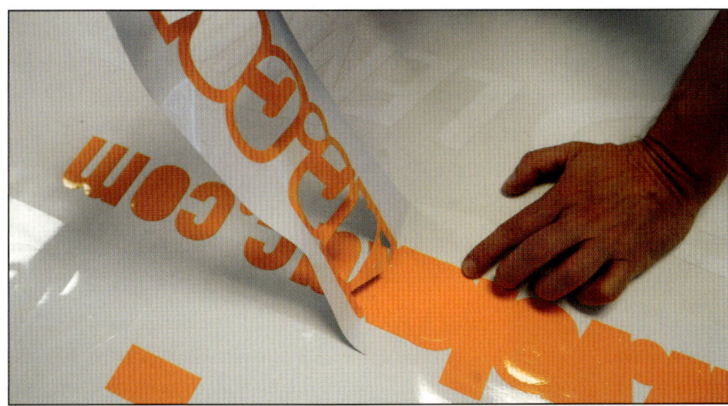

Once the machine has cut the graphics, remove all excess material. This process is called weeding. Make sure that the vinyl stays on its original backing. It can be helpful to use tweezers and a sewing needle to remove the small pieces of excess vinyl. With the "o" in "com," the vinyl in the middle needs to be removed to have a proper "o." It takes time, but there is not much of a learning curve to this step as long as you are careful. Slowly pull the excess material back and hold down the parts of what needs to stay.

We get our transfer film from Fellers. It comes in roll form just like vinyl. Make sure your transfer film has no creases in it on the roll or when you lay it on the film. True to its name, transfer film will transfer any creases.

keep the vehicle until the project is complete.

Never keep the client's vehicle during the production phase. If you have the measurements, there is no need to have the vehicle until the graphics have been created and are ready to be installed. It's unnecessary and will only add to the time that the client will be without the vehicle.

Once the graphics have been produced, prepare them to be applied to the vehicle prior to setting up the client's installation appointment. If the graphics were run through the plotter (a machine that cuts the vinyl to create certain aspects of the design, such as shapes and lettering) during production, you need to complete the weeding process, which is removing the unwanted sections from the graphic. Once this has been completed, you will have what looks like the exact same graphic that was mocked up. The graphic is ready for the final step in your production phase: applying the transfer film.

Applying Transfer Film to Graphics

Transfer film is a thin piece of material placed on top of the graphic before installation to make the positioning and application process simple and easy. The film is tacky on one side, sold by the roll, and offered in a various widths and lengths.

To apply the transfer film to the graphic, lay the graphic face up on a cutting table or any other clean, flat surface. Unroll enough transfer film to cover the entire graphic. If the graphic is long in length, have another person help so that each person can hold on to either end of the film.

Now that the proper amount of transfer film is unrolled, hover it a few feet directly above the graphic with the tacky side of the film facing down, and begin to lower the middle section of film until it makes contact with the graphic. Slowly lower each side of the transfer film down and allow it to gradually cover the remaining area of the graphic from the middle section out toward each end.

Using the same type of squeegee used to install vinyl wrap on a car, begin in the middle of the graphic and apply pressure to the top of the transfer film. Chase the air out from the middle of the graphic out toward the end. Go back to the middle and work the transfer film to complete the other end. Take your time. You do not want any trapped air or wrinkles in the transfer film. Once completed, the transfer film will be firmly adhered to the top of your graphic with a smooth surface throughout the entire area. A smooth surface will make your installation easier.

Pay attention during the squeegee process across the transfer film. If you accidentally trap air or set in a wrinkle, stop and lift the transfer to correct the section before moving on. You will be glad that you corrected the mistake at this point when it comes time to install.

The transfer film has now been laid over the designed, printed, laminated, and plotted graphic. The graphic has also been weeded. Just like wrapping a vehicle panel, make sure there is a perfect, flat installation of the transfer paper onto the graphic. Be careful to not reposition the transfer paper so the graphic is not pulled from the vinyl backing. Take the squeegee over the transfer film to make sure that all of the bubbles are out, and make sure that it sticks to the graphic. This is important.

Now that the graphic is covered with transfer film, cut away and discard any extra material on all four sides of the graphic. It's not required, but I prefer to use a straightedge when make these cuts. If the graphic is square or rectangular in nature, a straight cut is extremely helpful to make it level and when installing lettering or text.

If a graphic has a circular shape, I cut it freehand and try to create the same amount of spacing all the way around the graphic to make it easier when it comes time to position the graphic correctly during the installation.

Paper and Clear Transfer

There are two main types of transfer film available: paper and clear. Although they both serve the same basic purpose, they have different characteristics.

The paper transfer feels thicker and sturdier than the clear and holds up better when used in warmer temperatures. However, because it is so sturdy, it's best used when applying graphics to a flatter surface and is more difficult to work with when used on areas that are curved or contain recesses.

The clear transfer is a little more flexible, and although it does not like the heat as much, it adheres on a slight curve or recess better than the paper transfer film. A lot of people like the fact that they can see through the clear film, which helps them position the graphic easier (they can see exactly what it will look like on the surface of the vehicle).

Ultimately, it all comes down to whichever type of transfer film that the installer prefers. I personally prefer the clear type most of the time, but if you are new to the film, try out both to figure out the best one for you.

After the graphics are covered in transfer film, take a moment to refer back to your final mock-up sheet and go through each graphic to make sure that none are missing. I place a check mark next to each graphic on the sheet as I go through them all. Once you have each graphic accounted for, bring in the vehicle and begin the installation process.

Vinyl Graphics Installation

Congratulations! You have created your design, produced your graphics, covered your graphics with transfer film, and checked to make sure you have everything you need. It is now time for installation onto the vehicle.

In this section, we will guide you through the installation process step by step, discuss registration and how it is used to achieve proper positioning, and explain different installation techniques. You will discover that when you understand how to implement these methods, you will be able to perform amazing-looking graphic installations in a short period of time and have lots of fun in the process.

A graphic installation can be completed in a fraction of the time that it typically takes to wrap a whole car and has the potential to be just as rewarding.

Initial Positioning of Entire Graphics Set

In some instances, each separate graphic that comprises the full design is unique and different. However, in many cases, individual graphics may closely resemble others within the set.

For example, there may be multiple graphics that look identical at first glance, but because they were designed to go on specific areas of the vehicle, they may vary slightly in size. It's because of a situation such as this that you should use masking tape and mock up every single graphic in the group that will go onto the vehicle before jumping in and installing the first one.

You won't spend a lot of time with this step. You are simply trying to figure out where everything goes. Tape each graphic onto vehicle near where it should be, but don't be too concerned about getting them in their perfect location at the moment.

Once every graphic has been taped on the vehicle, compare the vehicle to the final mock-up. Make sure that every graphic is accounted for and that each one has been sized correctly. You are now ready to begin registering your first graphic for installation.

How to Register Graphics for Installation

When you register a graphic, you create a map that shows you precisely where to place the graphic during installation. There is no need to guess where the graphic goes, which helps free up the installer's mind to focus on the installation itself.

To begin the registration process, take four or five pieces of masking tape and lightly tack them to your shirt or arm so that they are within reach. Take your time and position the graphic in the precise location in which it needs to be according to your mock-up.

Next, place the masking tape in four or five spots along the edge of the graphic so that half of the tape is adhered to the graphic and the other half is adhered to the vehicle. Take your fingernail and create a line in the tape along the outside edge of the graphic. Using your knife, lightly run the blade along that line. Use caution during this step. Don't use too much pressure and cut through the tape and into the vehicle's clear coat.

If you are a novice and are new to using a blade on a vehicle's surface,

Green painter's tape has been used to position the graphic. Use key features of the vehicle to make sure that it appears as it does in the mock-up. Once the graphic is in the right place, hold it there with multiple pieces of tape. These pieces of tape act as guides when the graphic is positioned.

Carefully cut the tape line. The tape should be placed partially on the top of the transfer paper and partially on the vehicle.

Place a long piece of green tape under the halfway point of the graphic to hold it in place because all of the other tape lines will be cut. Peel the backing from the graphic. If you think of a sticker, this is the same style of backing that is peeled away. Don't peel away the graphic from the transfer film. This step needs to be done carefully so that the graphic stays on the transfer film.

perform one more step. Use a dry-chalk pen to make registration lines after you have positioned the graphic to be sure that the graphic is correctly placed.

Using masking tape for registration marks is the better method because it won't be erased during cleaning. Once each piece of tape has been cut, lift the graphic off and away from the vehicle. The graphic now has four or five pieces of tape around the edge that correspond to the pieces of tape that remain on the vehicle. When the graphic is placed in the correct position, those pieces of tape match up to one another perfectly.

Now that the graphic is off the car and all the registration marks are in place, go through the cleaning process to ensure that the surface area is prepped and ready for installation.

Installing a Graphic

The purpose of the transfer film that was applied on top of the graphic during production is to ensure that all of the pieces of the graphic stay in the right place during install. Once the vehicle's surface has been cleaned and the registration marks have been made, slowly peel the backing off of the graphic.

As the backing is removed, pay close attention that all areas of the graphic are sticking to the transfer film. If the graphic is complex and has a lot of small pieces, you may need to stop and go back and forth with the transfer to allow it to pick up pieces it missed on the first peel. Remember, transfer film works best when applied indoors in temperatures around 77°F.

In warmer temperatures, the film may become less tacky, and it could take several attempts until all pieces are successfully picked up by the film. When the backing has been fully removed and all pieces of the graphic are on the transfer film, it is time to place it onto the vehicle. For smaller graphics, they are easy to install with one person.

Register the graphic by matching the pieces of tape on the graphic with the pieces of tape on the vehicle. It is important to have the graphic taut, so pull on each end of the graphic when placing it. A graphic that is placed on the vehicle loosely will be difficult to install.

Once the graphic is placed onto the vehicle, apply pressure with a squeegee to ensure that all areas of the graphic are adhered to the vehicle. Take a moment to analyze the graphic and determine the best approach before you begin to squeegee the graphic down. Most graphics like to be installed from the top down, but, depending on the nature and size of the graphic, you may want to start in the middle and work out toward the edges.

If you are installing a large graphic, have another person assist you in the initial placement. Pull the graphic from each angle right before the graphic makes contact with the surface so there is a fair amount of tension on it as it goes down.

In the case of installing a large graphic that is too difficult to handle for one person and you do not have the luxury of having another installer around to help, incorporate what is referred to as the "hinge technique." This divides the graphic into two different sections and makes installation easier. To do this, place the graphic in its proper position on the vehicle and line up all the registration points.

Next, take a piece of masking tape that is longer than the graphic by about 6 or 7 inches on each side and run the tape through the middle of the graphic either vertically or horizontally (depending on the shape of the graphic). You have essentially split the size of the graphic half and can install each half separately. Lift one side of the graphic off of the vehicle, peel the backing, and then use a zippy tool (a plastic tool with a channel guide where you feed the material in to cut it) to cut the backing.

Using a squeegee, apply pressure and install half of the graphic onto the vehicle. Once you have that half installed, remove the long piece of tape. Peel the rest of the backing off the graphic and finish squeegeeing the second portion onto the vehicle.

Double Checking

After the graphic has been squeegeed onto to the surface, go over the entire area to ensure that all parts of the graphic have been applied. The edges of the graphic are sometimes missed. Slowly pull the transfer film up off the graphic. Use your fingers to tap down any areas that might not be completely adhered to the vehicle. Once all areas of the graphic are down, grab your heat gun and give the entire surface a good post heat.

You have just successfully laid the first graphic in your group set and are ready to install the rest. Remember, when it comes to positioning graphics that are made separately but are placed near each other, take your time to measure the distance between the two pieces. It is easy to make adjustments before locking in the registration points to ensure the final install looks as professional as possible.

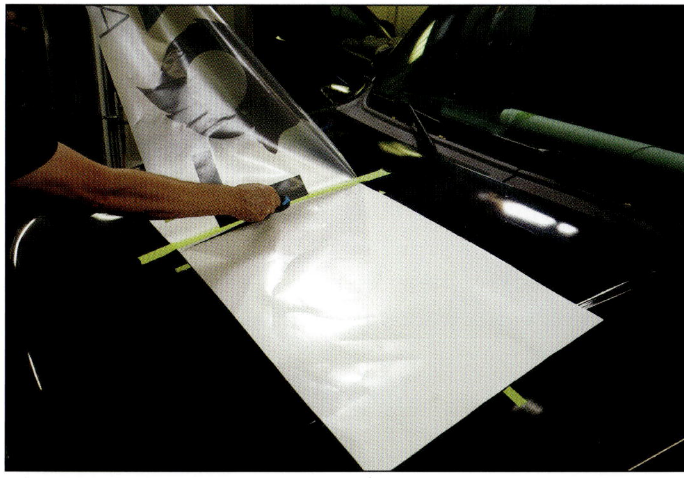

The backing has been peeled off up to the green tape line. Use a zippy tool to cut away the backing. This is so that the backing won't interfere with the installation. Notice that all of the tape lines are still on the vehicle to act as a guide as the film is placed back down.

Now that the backing is out of the way, place the graphic to match up with the tape lines. Now you can see why you went through all this. Use a squeegee to press hard on the graphic letters to make sure that the adhesive attaches to the vehicle. Transfer paper is sticky but not nearly as sticky as vinyl wrap. Once the adhesive is locked, it's not a huge task to pull away the transfer paper. Do it slowly and carefully to make sure that the graphic stays where it should.

The graphic is now attached to the vehicle's surface, and the transfer paper has been pulled away. Do a post-heat over the graphic to make sure that no bubbles come up.

VINYL WRAP CARE AND PROTECTION

The world of vinyl care is confusing to most people, and if it is not addressed properly, it will affect the life and look of the film. Various environments can affect the film, especially when proper care instructions are not followed.

Reasons to Keep Vinyl Clean

Vinyl works like a tractor beam for pollutants in the air. These pollutants attach to the film and stay until they are cleaned from the surface. When the pollutants interact with water, it can cause an acidic chemical reaction on the vehicle. Heat and acid create the perfect environment for the destruction of the wrap. This is especially important in environments with high pollution and morning dew. It can be surmised that acid is not a great substance to have sitting on your film.

Other outside factors, such as bird poop, can be bad to have sitting on the vinyl surface. It is for these reasons that the vehicle must be washed once a week to maintain the integrity of the product. It is also important to immediately remove any unwanted substance from the vinyl, such as gasoline, tire shine, bird poop, tree sap, etc. These are items that should be wiped off the moment that they touch the film.

How to Wash Vinyl Wrap

After years of telling people how to care for their wraps, we have boiled it down to one simple statement: treat it like a gloss black paint job.

We don't recommend going through a brush car wash or using an

Here's a full 3M 1080 Satin Grey wrap with gloss black accents on a BMW i8. All of the seams are hidden in the vehicle's natural panel breaks. If done correctly, the appearance should be identical to paint.

Do Not Wax Vinyl

3M does not recommend using wax on vehicle wraps. We have successfully used turtle black and other products on black gloss wraps. These wraps, just like vehicle paint, will always show light scratches. Since 3M does not recommend this wax, use great caution and use it only under circumstances of great distress. Usually, some time in the sun is enough to heal a lot of films. ■

3M Guidelines

- Wash whenever the car appears dirty. Contaminants allowed to remain on the graphic may be more difficult to remove during cleaning.
- Rinse off as much dirt and grit as possible with a spray of water.
- See Difficult Contaminants below for spot cleaning bird droppings, tar, etc.
- Use a wet, nonabrasive detergent, such as 3M Car Wash Soap 39000, Meguiar's NXT Generation Car Wash, or Deep Crystal Car Wash, and a soft, clean cloth or sponge.
- Rinse thoroughly with clean water. To reduce water spotting, immediately use a silicone squeegee to remove water and finish with a clean microfiber cloth

Spraying Vinyl

Spray the graphic or vinyl wrap directly. Holding the nozzle of a pressure washer at an angle to the graphic may lift the edges of the film. ■

abrasive cloth or harsh chemicals. In a perfect world, clients would hand wash the vehicle with a high-quality soap made for premium vehicle applications. This is the simple version.

Since many of the films we use are from 3M or Avery, we will talk about their official statements on how to clean your vehicle. These, after all, are the companies to contact to discuss any sort of warranty issues.

Above is the official 3M statement on maintaining its films. This information can also be found at 3M.com.

Automated Car Washes

Car washes are okay, but only if it is a touchless wash. It is not recommended to use a brush car wash. We don't even recommend brush washes on OEM paint. I wrapped my vehicle and took it through a brush wash for years, mostly as a test to the film. It did not cause any major visible impact, but it did make the removal down the road more difficult. My advice is to avoid them. I will always recommend a hand wash over a car wash.

Pressure Washing

Although hand washing is the preferred cleaning method, pressure washing may be used under these conditions.

- Water pressure below 2,000 psi (14 MPa)
- Water temperature below 180°F (80°C)
- Use a spray nozzle with a 40-degree wide-angle spray pattern
- Keep the nozzle at least 1 foot (300 mm) away from the vehicle and perpendicular (at 90°) to the graphic

Difficult Contaminants

Soften difficult contaminants, such as bug splatter, bird droppings, tree sap, and similar contaminants, by soaking them for several minutes with hot, soapy water. Rinse it thoroughly and dry. If further cleaning is needed, test Meguiar's Gold Class Bug and Tar Remover or 3M Citrus Base Cleaner in an inconspicuous area to ensure that there is no damage to the graphics. Diluted isopropyl alcohol (2 parts alcohol to 1 part water) or denatured alcohol may also help. Spot-clean the contaminants.

Do not use rough scrubbing or abrasive tools that will scratch the film. Wash and rinse all residue immediately.

Washing Methods to Avoid

Avoid heavy-brush car washes. We do not advise these for any vehicle that one cares about, let alone a wrapped vehicle. It is important to think about what brushes or pieces of fabric can do to a vehicle. Often, these fabric pieces contain abrasive dirt that hits and scratches the vehicle over and over.

High-pressure power washing should be avoided. Power washing itself is fine at a low pressure and at least a foot away, but don't point the nozzle right at a corner or seam of the wrap. Do not let this scare you from using a power washer in general. There is nothing wrong with it, but be careful.

Clean or new microfiber cloths are highly recommended to wash and to dry the vehicle before spots can occur. If water spots bake onto the vehicle, they can be difficult to remove—just as with any paint job.

Fuel Spills

Wipe off any fuel spill immediately to avoid degrading the vinyl and adhesive. Then wash, rinse, and dry the vehicle as soon as possible.

Care for the vehicle's graphics like you would any fine paint finish. Using high-quality 3M products designed specifically for car care and these cleaning and maintenance procedures will help keep your 3M graphics looking their best.

Film Restoration

The following restoration recommendations will keep your vehicle wraps looking their best:

- Do not use any abrasive polishes or cutting compounds.
- Do not use any polishing or wax products on matte or textured films.
- If there is wax or wax residue on the surface, remove it with an all-purpose cleaner. ■

Ceramic Coatings and Sealants

Think of vinyl like your skin. The first thing your skin does when exposed to the sun for a long period of time is dehydrate. Once your skin is dry, it is easier for the sun to burn your skin. Film works the same way. When it is dried out, it will start to burn. This is a reason that a proper sealant or coating can be useful.

We have also mentioned several outside forces that must be addressed for keeping the integrity of the film. The fear of some of these occurrences can be greatly deescalated with clear coating. Bird poop, gasoline, and other awful outside influences will not have near as much of an impact as the sun. However, they should be wiped clean as quickly as possible.

Ceramic coatings are all the rage in the premium vehicle world. It is a great way to protect your paint from scratching as well as make it easy to clean a vehicle. Many products offer UV protection and are hydrophobic to bead off liquids. These are great qualities for the wrap as well. Luckily, there are several brands on the market that make ceramic coatings specifically to protect vinyl wrap. The brand that we use and trust is called Waxed Shine. It carries a line of paint and vinyl-only protectants.

These coatings can help combat the age escalation that the sun elicits and allow troublesome things such as bird poop to be wiped away. Adding a ceramic coating to the vehicle is like the candy shell on an M&M and offers a first level of protection that boosts the longevity of the wrap. Many manufacturers make specialty products for matte, gloss, and satin films. Make sure to choose the right one. Otherwise, you can risk losing the finish. Since matte products tend to dehydrate much quicker than others, it is wise to add this product in harsh environments like Arizona. As previously mentioned, dehydration quickly leads to burning, which then leads to a dull and cracked wrap.

If you don't want to go to the expense or time of using a ceramic product, sealant is a great alternative. Sealants allow for some protection from scratches as well as a hydration/UV protectant quality. Once again, some type of treatment is highly recommended, especially with matte films.

If you choose to further protect the vinyl with a coating product, Waxed Shine has two general product offerings for this type of job. If you have a matte or satin vinyl, use Top Coat. If your vinyl is gloss, use T+SiO2 Titanium Coating. Just like vinyl wrap, have a clean and well-lit location to apply this product.

Gloss Vinyl Coating

Waxed Shine makes an incredible product (T+SiO2 Titanium Coating) for vehicle wrap and paint protection. It is the only product of its type to have a self-healing coating. Make sure to use a clean rag on the wrap to prevent scratches. Use Waxed Shine products and a bit of heat to remove scratches. For increased longevity and ease of cleaning, a coating is a great addition to a vehicle's wrap.

Applying a Vinyl Wrap Protective Coating

1 *A waxed-shine ceramic-coating kit comes with a block applicator and cloth, distribution tube, and product. This product must be purchased through a reputable dealer or directly from Waxed Shine. Vinyl experts are realizing that more and more protection is paramount to make wraps last. Some people have a hard time realizing that a wrap, paint, or other product needs to be treated with care.*

2 Waxed Shine's panel prep cleaner can be used to prepare vehicle paint for vinyl. It will remove oil and fingerprints and is recommended for the best possible finish in tandem with their product. Use a set of rubber gloves for this entire process.

3 Shake the bottle just before use. Latex gloves are important for keeping the work clean. Shaking the product for just under a minute is sufficient.

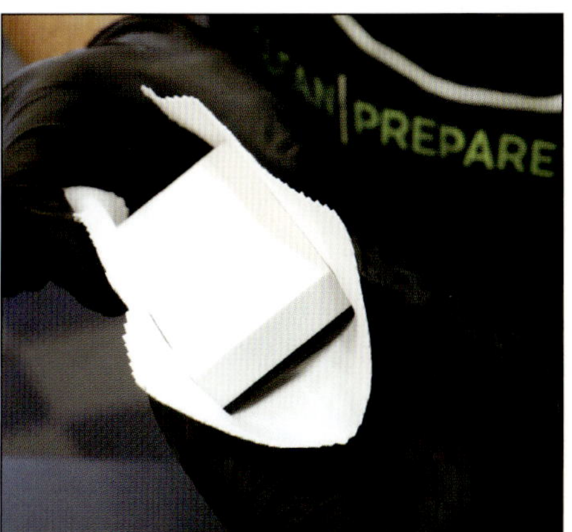

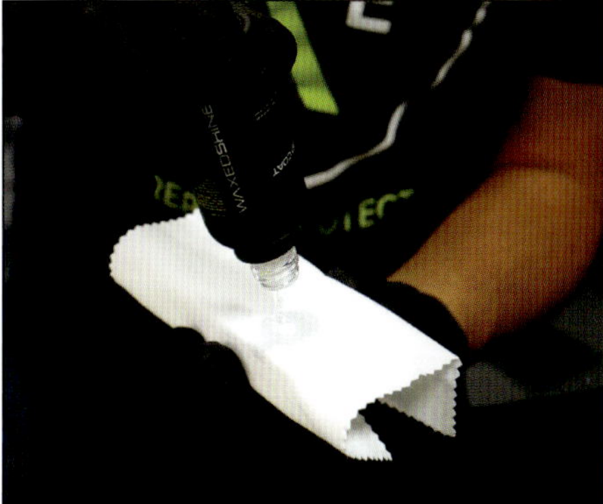

4 Wrapping the cloth around the application block allows for an even application process. If you apply it by hand, various pressures are applied unevenly at various times. Since the products are time sensitive and set in permanently, it's important to have an even and well-placed coating.

5 Use the distribution tube or go straight from the bottle to apply a healthy layer of product to ensure that the cloth is fully covered. It shouldn't be soaking wet, but there shouldn't be dry patches. After the coating is applied to each section, immediately use a clean microfiber towel to remove any excess product.

6 Apply the coating in straight lines from north to south until the entire section is coated. Overlap each stroke by an inch to ensure that the coverage is even and fully distributed. Apply this to no more than a 4x4-foot section at any given time.

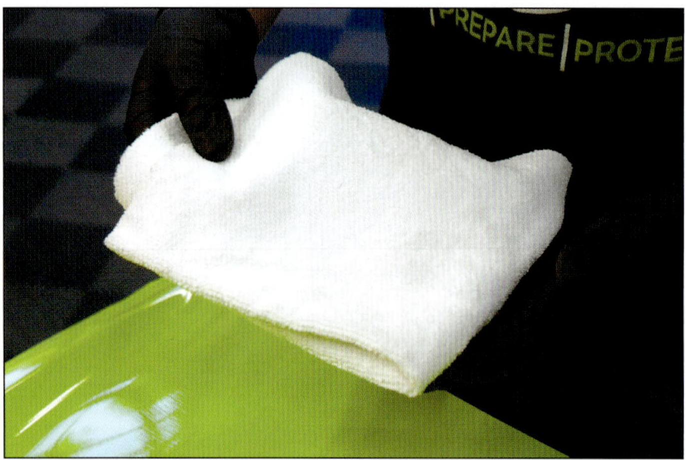

7 *This is the microfiber cloth that is recommended. It is perfect for this job.*

8 *Immediately after the coating has been applied to each section, use a clean microfiber cloth to remove any excess product. After this step, allow the coating to dry for 24 hours. Don't drive the vehicle; it should be parked in as clean of an area as possible. Dust attaches to the coating, so vehicles that are parked in dusty areas feel like sandpaper after the coating has cured. The vehicle will have a perfectly smooth surface after 24 hours if everything was done correctly.*

9 *We have addressed how to protect gloss surfaces, but many people wrap a cars with matte or satin. These wraps are even harder to care for than gloss. We suggest the Waxed Shine top coat product to protect these finishes. Matte and satin films dehydrate in the sun quicker, which speeds up their life span. In my opinion, they are even more important to protect than a gloss vinyl film. Shake the bottle immediately before use.*

10 *This product has the same setup as the other product, but the inside of the bottle has a different chemical composition and can be used on other surface types. Clean and prep vinyl as previously mentioned, or use Waxed Shine panel prep cleaner. It will remove oil and fingerprints and is recommended for the best possible finish when used in tandem with their product. Use rubber gloves for this entire process.*

11 *Don't forget to shake the bottle for about a minute immediately before use.*

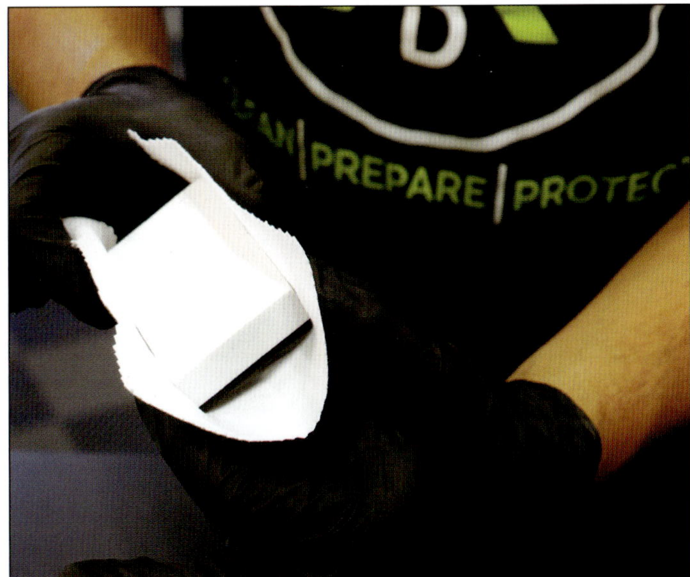
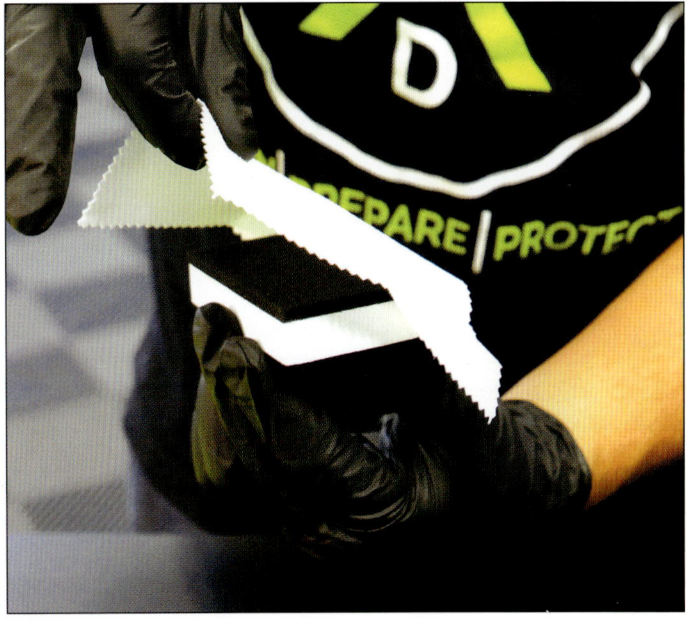

12 *Wrap the cloth around the application block. Make sure that the cloth is 100 percent clean and free of debris.*

13 *Wrap the black side of the block.*

14 *Open the bottle and evenly pour the coating over entire facing surface on the applicator.*

15 *Apply the coating in straight lines from north to south until the entire section is coated. Overlap each stroke an inch to ensure that the coverage is even and fully distributed. Apply no more than a 4x4-foot section at any given time.*

16 *Notice how the products work on a different surface. Wetting the material causes a sheen on the matte finish.*

17 *Hold the block like this to get as large of a surface distribution as possible and not overcoat.*

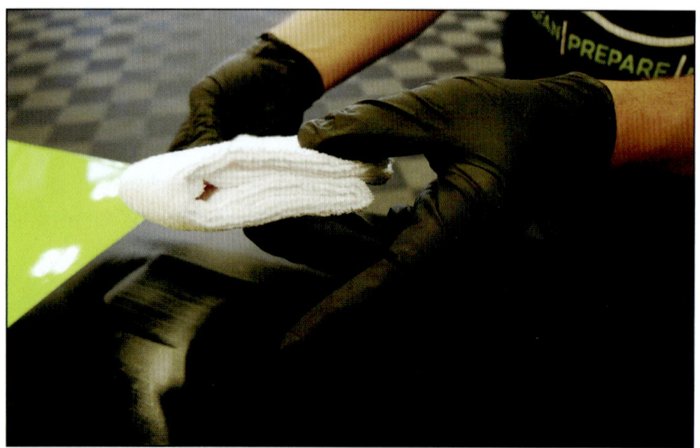

18 *After the coating has been applied to each section, immediately use a clean microfiber cloth to remove any excess coating product. The vinyl will return to a darker matte finish.*

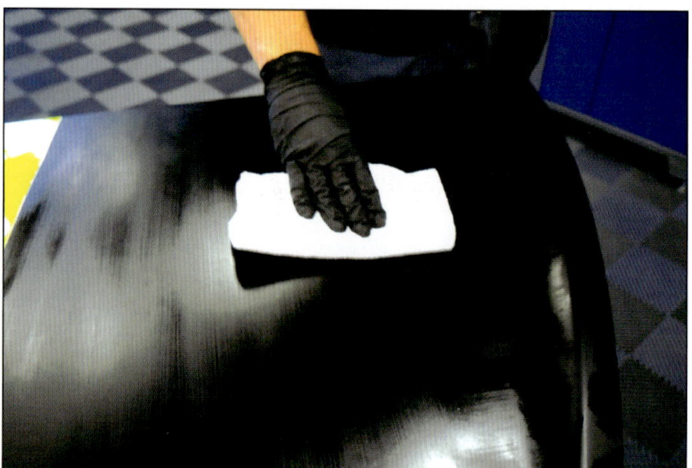

19 *Notice how the entire surface had a wet appearance but slowly fades away as the excess residue is removed and the surface dries.*

20 *Some may get nervous to see a sheen on the matte surface during application. After the 24-hour cure time, it will be back to the base finish, be easier to take care of, and last longer. It's important to research products before trying them. Waxed Shine has a great team, and we suggest a chat with this company regarding a particular project before coating. This is a fast-moving, innovative industry, and things are always changing.*